Gay Fathers

GAY FATHERS

ROBERT L. BARRET

BRYAN E. ROBINSON

Lexington Books

D.C. Heath and Company • Lexington, Massachusetts • Toronto

Library of Congress Cataloging-in-Publication Data

Barret, Robert L.
Gay fathers / Robert L. Barret, Bryan E. Robinson.
p.   cm.
ISBN 0-669-19514-6 (alk. paper)
1. Gay fathers—Counseling of—United States.   2. Gay fathers—
United States.   I. Robinson, Bryan E.   II. Title.
HQ76.2.U5B37   1990
306.847'2—dc20   90-32417
CIP

Published simultaneously in Canada.
Printed in the United States of America.
Casebound International Standard Book Number: 0–669–19514–6
Library of Congress Catalog Card Number: 90–32417

The paper used in this publication meets the minimum requirements of
American National Standard for Information Sciences—Permanence
of Paper for Printed Library Materials, ANSI Z39.48–1984.

Year and number of this printing:

92 93 94 8 7 6 5 4 3 2

This book is dedicated to gay fathers,
and their children, parents, wives, brothers, and sisters;
who are developing alternative lifestyles
that affirm the rich potential of gay parenting.

Contents

Figures, Tables, and Boxes

Figure

Tables

Boxes

Preface

I N our work with fathers over the past ten years, we became aware of the need for a book that helps gay fathers, their children and families, and the practitioners who interact with them to understand the various dilemmas they face. The notion of integrating both fatherhood and homosexuality frequently seems impossible to all involved in what is a unique and complicated process.

The wives, parents, brothers, sisters, and children of gay fathers often find themselves in a bewildering array of emotionally charged situations that appear overwhelming and impossible to resolve. Rather than focus on the all too familiar negative aspects of this family situation, there is a need for material that presents the full range of positive and negative life experiences these families encounter. What emerged is a book that presents rich and authentic case material that illustrates the personal and parental complications that arise when gay men have children. Questions and concerns are addressed for family-life educators, family therapists, public-health workers, nurses, physicians, health educators, counselors, caseworkers, the clergy, psychologists, teachers, and family members who participate in this intense drama.

This book is a synthesis of our work with many gay fathers and shows how complicated and unique each situation is. It combines scientific knowledge with actual case studies drawn from in-depth interviews, our private counseling practice, and from our original research.

Gay men with children find themselves with numerous dilemmas in an atmosphere that typically offers little support and understanding to either their father role or their gayness. Chapter one gives an overview of some of the personal and legal issues that accompany gay fatherhood and an important examination of issues related to psychotherapy with gay men. Building on that base, chapter two examines the myths and realities associated with how gay fathers are viewed by friends, family members, and society in general. In chapter three we present the many different configurations gay fatherhood takes, and we discuss the effects on their children in chapter four. In chapter five we discuss gay fathering vis à vis the father's relationship with his parents and wife. We cover the impact of HIV disease on gay fathering in chapter six, and go on to discuss the many barriers confronting social scientists as they attempt to study these men and their complicated family lives in chapter seven. Finally the appendix contains an extensive list of books, audiovisual aids, support organizations, and other resources for those interested in further reading or study to strengthen their helping skills. Each chapter concludes with tips for practitioners on how to approach and resolve the many difficulties gay fathers and their families face.

This book is an outgrowth of our desire to put the topic of gay fatherhood in its proper perspective, to debunk the many stereotypes associated with gay fathers, and to improve services to them. It is also intended to challenge the notion that gay fathers and their children, wives, and parents are ultimately victimized by homosexuality. Presenting gay fatherhood as an opportunity to teach others about the richness, diversity, and strengths inherent in gay communities as part of the movement to combat homophobia is another not-so-subtle agenda. As we have listened to many gay fathers tell of their experiences, we are struck by their courage and internal beliefs as they build strong family units in social systems that rarely provide support and understanding. Hopefully, this book will enhance the success of gay men who are parents.

Acknowledgments

W E have many people to thank for making this book possible. Our colleagues at the University of Georgia and the
University of North Carolina at Charlotte have provided encouragement and moral and administrative support. Dr. Patsy
Skeen and Dr. Lynda Walters were investigators in two of the
national studies discussed at length in this book. They were in-
strumental in designing and implementing much of the original
research upon which we report. Dr. Mary Thomas Burke, Chair
of the Department of Human Services, and Dr. Harold Heller,
Dean of the College of Education and Allied Professions at the
University of North Carolina at Charlotte provided their usual
unyielding support.

We thank Lauren Stayer for her expert help in manuscript
preparation and Lorraine Penninger for hours of time on com-
puter searches and other library support. We extend our heart-
felt thanks to Dennis Stabler, Charles Watrous, Henry Finch,
Tim Alwran, Colin Johnson, Michael Finch, Rex Vinyl, Mark
Drum, Chip Drum, and Callie Drum as well as to all the anonymous gay fathers, their parents, and children who contributed
case material for this book.

1

Counseling Gay Fathers
Social and Cultural Factors

THE CASE OF SAM

I wondered if I was gay off and on for years. But most of the people I met who seemed to be gay (or at least were taunted by being called "queer") were real different from me. I suppose I just fell into doing what was expected. Looking back now, I can tell that I was scared of my homosexual feelings and tried to convince myself they were not important. So, in high school and college I went out with girls, and I got married as soon as I finished college, convinced that was the best way to do away with my sexual attraction toward men. Like most young couples in the 1960s, it was not long before the children came along, and I was toiling away as the breadwinner to provide for the needs of my wife, son, and daughter. As distracting as that pressure was, I still had fantasies about being sexually involved with men, but I was determined not to let them become real.

Over the years I really got into the father thing. I loved watching my children grow up, teaching them to ride bikes, enjoying the out of doors, playing sports . . . all the things that fathers can do with their children. I sat through lots of music and dance recitals and interacted with teachers and scout leaders just like all parents. Naturally, those demands got "old" at times, but today I miss them. So much of my identity as an adult was tied up in being a father. One of the hardest things about finally identifying as a gay man has been leaving the family that I helped create. Oh, sure, I see my kids often, and I know they love me, but living as a gay man has placed a particular burden on all of us, and sometimes I probably hang back as a father for fear that I am hurting my kids in some perverse way.

Our family seemed to work even though my wife and I became more friends than lovers. We continued to have sex fairly regularly, although neither of us was ever really totally excited about it. Sex was pleasurable, but not nearly as dynamic as I thought it could be. We loved each other and created a family in which each person was free to pursue individual interests and one that acknowledged the core commitment that we had for each other. At the same time, I came to feel more and more isolated as I struggled with the deception that I was living before the three people that I loved the most. And finally, as the kids went off to college, I knew I had to resolve my sexuality once and for all.

The first person I told was my wife. We knew we were at a point where we needed to make some changes in our relationship, and I saw myself about to recommit to the marriage (which basically was deciding to live "the lie" for the rest of my life) or to make a radical change that would have major consequences for all of us. She seemed very understanding at first and admitted that she had wondered if I might be gay. We agreed that I would begin to make contacts in the gay community and explore my feelings, but that I would not become sexually involved with anyone.

Being gay is definitely more than having sex with men. I learned that the "gay lifestyle" is really a myth. There is just as much diversity among gay men as among any group. But the fundamental issue (beyond erotic feelings) is that there are negative consequences to living as a gay man. Not only did I have to face my own homophobia as I tried to accept myself as gay, but I also had to figure out how to integrate my gay friends and activities into my professional and social life. Many people can deal with gay men abstractly, but having a friend who is gay is another matter altogether. My straight friends didn't reject me outright, but I could tell that they were struggling to be comfortable with me. It seemed that all they could think about was my sexual activity, and it was obvious that they, like most people, had a problem with that. It was strange because at first there was so little sexual contact with men.

I was determined that I would not sneak around and constantly hide the fact that I was gay. I was not sure how that would go for me, and I lived in fear of the hurt I knew my children would experience when they learned that I was gay.

It seems like only yesterday that I told the children about me. We all cried, and for several weeks they did not want to have anything to do with me. My daughter told me that she didn't want to know this about me and that she would never discuss it with me again. That has created a major strain in our relationship. I'm not very good about making small talk and leaving out the details of my life with her. When I asked her if she would be willing to meet some of my new friends, she replied angrily, "Dad, that will never happen." That hurt me a lot. I haven't given up though, and I hope the day will come when she will be able to accept me as I am. She did write to me and thanked me for being such a good father to her. She mentioned the values I had taught her and the way I had helped her over the years. "One thing's for sure," she wrote, "you have been a great father and I'm proud to be your daughter." I know she loves me, and I enjoy hearing about her work and the life she is making with her husband. I don't know what will happen when they have children. Sometimes I worry that they will not be comfortable having me around; other times I just trust that things will work out.

My son has been a complete surprise to me. He was quiet for a few weeks, but then he called me one night and said, "You know, you will always be my dad." I cried when we hung up . . . not just because I was touched by what he had said, but also because I knew the risk he was taking in facing his own feelings about me. Since then, we've had a few good talks about it, and he's met some of my friends. It is clear that he is not gay, and I'm happy about that for him. Next Christmas he and his wife are coming to be with me. I suppose we're all nervous about that, but we're also determined to work through the issues that will inevitably come up. I'm not in a relationship yet; that may be the real test of how the family will accept me. Time will tell about that.

There are times when I feel sad that I hid my sexuality for so long. Other times I am angry about being gay and wish I could do something to go back to the secure, traditional family life I once had. But I refuse to live a lie—that's no longer possible for me. And I'm actually proud about being a gay man most of the time. I was born this way, and now I realize that I can be proud of who I am, and that includes affirming the ways being gay enable me to make a contribution to my children and friends.

Well, we're not exactly the Smith family next door. There are times I know my story sounds like a soap opera. I wish it sounded more normal and that people in general could understand that we are doing the best we can in a situation that is not always easy. I have moved across the country, but I am still in touch with my ex-wife and talk to my kids each week. My parents and sisters seem okay with all of this, but I think everyone is relieved that I am living far away and they don't have to deal with me on a daily basis. I know I am happier than I've ever been even though living alone is not fun. My son said to me the other day, "Dad, I can tell that you are so happy now. That's what's important, and if this is bringing that to you, then I'm all for it!" Wow! What a gift that was. I have learned that each of us has an adjustment to make as I make this new life for myself. I believe that if I can learn to love myself, the family will also learn to love me more fully. At least, that's what I hope will happen.

It was not too long ago that the idea of a man being both gay and a father seemed like a contradiction in terms. It was not just that people thought gay men incapable of having sex with women, but also that the notion of them as good and loving parents clashed with the stereotype of gay men. But today, more and more gay fathers are coming out of the closet to their families, and many of them are creating successful relationships with their children and proving that they can be more than just adequate parents. Part of their visibility results from the public custody suits many of them courageously undertake in order to have their parental rights guaranteed. Gay fathers have also become more visible as part of the new attention that has been devoted to fathering in general. Before the 1970s, the idea of a single father having custody of his children was viewed as unusual and not in the best interests of the child. Fortunately, today we now know that fathers make good "mothers" too, and virtually all elements of society have come to acknowledge the unique role that fathering plays in child development.

This chapter will present a review of the legal issues facing gay fathers, their motivations to become parents, and some of the issues that a mental health professional may anticipate when working with gay fathers. Legal issues are fundamental in understanding the obstacles that our government has created to prevent gay fathers from having access to their children. Even though this situation is changing across the country, the legal system stands as a formidable foe against most gay fathers.

Gay Rights and the Legal System

In 1969, gay men reacting against indiscriminate brutality fought back the New York police who were harassing them. The Stonewall riot that followed is seen as the beginning of the gay liberation movement. Looking back twenty years later, it is obvious that there have been significant gains as gay men and lesbians have used the courts and public opinion to gain access to the rights that many take for granted. In spite of the stubborn persistence of the negative stereotype of gay people, many have come to view homosexuals as nonthreatening, productive men and women who want to add to the stability of their communities.

At times, the gay literature has often not served this movement very well. Terms such as "faggots," "fairies," "queens," and "marys" are used freely both outside of and within the gay culture. Too often, the gay press has exploited gay men and lesbians by depicting them as victims of oppression who deserve special attention. Although the image of victims may be helpful in arousing public sympathy, too often members of the "victim" group may acquire the negative association with self as victim rather than a more positive notion of self as empowered and able to function successfully in the larger social system. The AIDS crisis has furthered the negative gay identity as the media refers to "AIDS victims" (most of whom we all know are homosexual men). It is certainly true that gay men and lesbians face discrimination in their personal and professional lives and that the public is not often sympathetic to their situation, leaving them to claim their rights through the legal system. Their success in legally won roles has caused many to view gay men and lesbians in a more positive light.

Issues of father custody in divorce cases have received attention in recent years as more and more men seek a fathering role that guarantees their participation in decisions about their children. Whereas the legal doors are opening more fully to fathers, an analysis of California court data from the 1970s reveals that the legal climate for father custody has not improved much (Weitzman & Dixon, 1979). Both judges and attorneys believed that maternal preference was practiced by the courts, and 48 percent of the lawyers stated that they would try to talk men out of seeking legal custody because they probably would not prevail. In such an unfavorable climate for fathers in general, it is highly unlikely that a gay man would stand much of a chance in the courts. Although research has shown that the father's homosexuality has little impact on the development of his children's sexual identity, courts are reluctant to place children in their care. A double standard has evolved in the legal system. Heterosexual couples are presumed to manage the expression of their sexuality in appropriate ways while gay fathers are assumed to flaunt their sexuality before their innocent children (Walters & Elam, 1985).

In 1987, Ron Carter (not his real name) was dying from AIDS and knew he had only months to live. His ex-wife refused to allow him to see his son, even though the father-son relationship had been strong and close. In spite of the debilitating impact of his illness, Ron chose to sue for custody in the courts; he wanted to spend as much of his remaining time as possible with his son. Fortunately, there are gay and lesbian rights organizations that exist to assist individuals who want to undertake the kind of battle that is demanded when one goes to court (see Appendix for a detailed list). Ron found his support from the National Center for Lesbian Rights, an organization that has assisted virtually every gay man or lesbian who has used the court to gain access to their children. In the end, the courts agreed, and Ron and his twelve-year-old son lived together for a full year before Ron's death.

Other gay men have used the courts to gain their rights to active parenting. In some of these cases, the courts somewhat reluctantly award custody to fathers because it is clear that the mother is unfit. In others, courts carefully choose between two suitable parents, and more and more frequently they will either award sole or joint custody to gay men. In some of these cases homosexual teenagers who have either run away from or been abandoned by their families have been placed with gay foster parents who are able to provide a positive model of gay relationships (Harry, 1983).

Most state courts, however, continue to base their decisions on myth and the negative stereotype of gay men. Their views are augmented by the claims of more conservative groups who see the gay rights movement as antifamily. For example, in 1989, voters in San Francisco were asked to enact a domestic partners law that would enable homosexuals to extend their employee benefits to their lovers. Assailed by conservative main-line religious groups as a direct threat to the family, this law, which would have enabled gay men and lesbians to include their partners on health insurance plans and provide emergency or sick leave when the partner was ill, was ultimately defeated.

This antifamily bias is frequently bolstered by the recommendations of social workers, juvenile parole officers, psychiatrists, psychologists, and other professionals who harbor negative attitudes about homosexuals. *Homophobia,* or fear of homosexuals, is a deeply ingrained and often subtle attitude that undermines our ability to see gay men and lesbians as people. It has been suggested that such attitudes are really more reflective of a homosexual hatred that will change only through a direct, aggressive, positive public relations campaign carefully designed to allay the public's fears of gay men and lesbians (Kirk & Madsen, 1989). In the meantime, courts continue to make decisions on the basis of supporting a model of the traditional family that may no longer exist. In cases in which gay men are biological fathers, it is almost impossible for them to secure custody or even visitation rights (Hitchens, 1980). Such denial of contact with their children is frequently based on the "immoral and unacceptable" character of homosexuals. A particular problem is that in many states, sexual intercourse between two men is still against the law, and courts find themselves in a bind when awarding custody of a minor to a father who openly lives with another man. This issue is often addressed when courts award custody but admonish gay fathers not to include their children in a gay lifestyle. For example, in New York, the ruling in the case of *Gottlieb vs. Gottlieb* warned the gay father not to expose his children to other gay friends or to take them to places where homosexuals might be present (Fadiman, 1983). Some gay fathers are learning that in order to act as fathers, they must once again slip back into the oppression of a closeted lifestyle. Whereas it is clear that these efforts have not met with complete success, the visibility of openly gay communities in major metropolitan areas has refuted the negative stereotype of gay men as irresponsible, sex-crazed, flamboyant clowns.

Changes do seem to be coming. In Washington, D.C., Massachusetts, and California, public policy forbids discrimination based on affectional or sexual orientations in foster care and custody decisions. And recent favorable court decisions affirming the rights of gay men and lesbians to adopt children are creating legal precedents that may have significant impact across the country (Herscher, 1989).

Living on the Fringe

Being a successful parent is not easy for any father, but being a successful gay father is even more difficult. Gay men are victimized by both heterosexual and homosexual worlds and often by their families, former spouses, and children. Studies show that 44 percent of gay fathers say they have been discriminated against because of their homosexuality. Examples cited were job loss, a job setback, social ostracism, name-calling, loss of housing, and subtle negativism. Heterosexuals generally consider homosexual fathers to be strange. Some think the terms "gay" and "father" are mutually exclusive, failing to understand why a homosexual man would marry or want to be a parent. Although not generally borne out by research findings, gay fathers are accused of marrying and parenting only to hide their homosexuality. As we discuss later, heterosexual society suspects gay fathers of child molestation, causing blurred sexual identity in their children (Marciano, 1985), providing a poor home environment, and subjecting their children to stigmatization.

Gay fathers are a minority within a minority. Although children represent status in the heterosexual world, they are a stigma not easily accepted by homosexuals (Bozett, 1984). As one gay man told us after he had met a father with three sons, "No thanks. I don't want to get involved with him. My life is complicated enough. I surely can't compete with that." The homosexual singles world does not easily accept "diaper talk," PTA meetings, and early departures from social events to relieve the baby sitter (Fadiman, 1983). The singles-oriented homosexual community is not used to children, and some find they prefer not to have children around and resent their interference with independence unless the child is emancipated or the gay father advocates his parental responsibilities. They find it difficult to cope with how completely children can captivate a parent (Maddox, 1982).

Children are also proof of heterosexual activity, and some gay men find that unacceptable. The gay partner may also resent the child, or there may be competition between partner and child, as one father told us:

> Both Hunter and my son became jealous of my attention. I felt torn between the two; each person seemed to demand more of my time than I was able to give. This was an irritant in my relationship with Hunter, a relationship that already lacked focus. Four months into the school year, our relationship had almost completely broken down. We still occupied the same apartment, but our love for each other, which we had openly shared with my son, had turned to hostility. My son perceived this hostility and became protective of me, and I felt defensive about his habits, which I knew bothered Hunter. I also felt jealous of their mutual enjoyment of boating.

Gay fathers who are married are victims of more divided identity. As the need to express their homosexuality becomes stronger over time, marriages are sure to run into difficulties. Wives often do not know of the husband's homosexuality, particularly since many of the husbands only gradually become aware of their homosexuality after marriage. Some couples stay together "for the sake of the children," perhaps giving the husband one night "out with the boys," or the husband may try to suppress his homosexuality. Others divorce or separate, which typically leads to disputes about the children's lives and what role the gay father and his lover will play in the lives of the children.

Gay fathers are marginal beings, caught between homosexual and heterosexual worlds. The nature of their marginality causes an intense need to reconcile these dualities. Yet gains in one world usually result in losses in the other. Inability to satisfy two standards of behavior results in alienation, loss of self-esteem, helplessness, and frustration. It is apparent that gay fathers must learn to cope with rejection and isolation from both homosexual and heterosexual worlds. As marginal beings, finding a place to fit in can be extremely frustrating. Social scientists recognize that gay fathers are victims of both homosexual and heterosexual worlds because they have two identities that are at opposite extremes of social acceptance (Bozett, 1983). Research suggests that gay fathers must resolve the disparity between their homosexual feelings and heterosexual behaviors. Gay fathers live in what has been dubbed "a double closet." The first closet is left behind when their homosexuality is disclosed and the second when their fatherhood is revealed to other homosexuals (Bozett, 1984; Fadiman, 1983).

Few research studies provide information about the impact of gay fathering on either the father or children. This neglect partially is reflective of the general neglect of the subject of fathering by scholars (Pleck & Sawyer, 1974), but also of the difficulty in finding subjects to participate in well controlled studies (Robinson & Barret, 1986). Undertaking a costly and emotionally draining court battle is not a project taken on whimsically. Those gay men and lesbians who brave such an undertaking are slowly changing a system that has all too often been indifferent to gay rights.

Reconciling Dual Identities

Once married, resentful feelings often emerge due to infrequent sexual contact between gay men and their spouses and feelings on the part of the spouses of having been deceived at the time of marriage (Ross, 1972). Many gay fathers begin to experience conflict between their duality of homosexual feelings and heterosexual status of fatherhood and seek to reconcile this conflict. Findings from a sample of eighteen gay fathers in San Francisco suggest that gay fathers have two identities that are opposite extremes (Bozett, 1981a, 1981b). On the one hand is the negative identity of homosexuality and on the other is the positive identity of fatherhood. The major tasks for gay fathers are to merge the two conflicting identities and to resolve the disparity between homosexual feelings and heterosexual behaviors. This is accomplished by a five-stage progression through (a) the period before marriage when the man is dating women, (b) marriage, (c) fatherhood, (d) alteration in the spousal relationship, usually separation and divorce, and (e) free activation of a homosexual lifestyle. This research indicates that gay fathers who were homosexually active before marriage tended to have an easier time reconciling their gay and father identities than those who were not.

Other interviews indicate that former gay husbands had been satisfied with their marriages and the majority (65.6 percent) considered the basic problem in their marriages to be the presence or emergence of their homosexuality, not incompatibility (Wyers, 1987). The impact of divorce and separation was more devastating to these men's wives than to the men themselves, although divorced gay fathers experienced a range of emotions from identity confusion, guilt, relief, and excitement to depression and loss.

Such a transition generates significant personal change. Brian Miller (1978) reported that the thirty gay husbands he interviewed went through an adolescent-like sexual reawakening and resocialization as they began to affirm their homosexuality.

> Homosexually oriented husbands tend to move from covert highly compartmentalized lifestyles, with all the surface appearances of suburban matrimonial accommodation, toward open, often militant, gay stances. Although ruptured marriages are left in the wake of this movement, these men consistently maintain commitment to and responsibility for their children, insofar as the courts allow. Such resocialization and consequent adjustments to life in a differing cultural milieu are seen as resulting not only from a complex process of negotiating, in which cognitive dissonance is resolved, but also from the

initiation of a homosexual love relationship. The latter appears
stronger than any other factor in enabling the husband to reas-
sess the potentialities of gay lifestyles and identities (p. 229).

Miller (1979b) also found that when gay men leave their
spouses and acquire a homosexual lifestyle, they experience an
enhanced self-esteem and a disappearance of psychosomatic ail-
ments (such as headaches, ulcers, and fatigue). Our case reports
support these findings indicating the father's emotional relief
from having to restrain his true self. After separation from their
spouses, many gay men also report that their gay relationships
are more harmonious than during their heterosexual marriages
and that fathering is more important and fulfilling than ever.

The disparity between their feelings (homosexual) and their
behavior (heterosexual) will lead many of these men to seek the
support of mental health services. Gay men who were active homosexuals prior to their marriages tended to make this transition with less emotional distress than those who had been closeted. The hurdles implicit in the gay father's development of a
positive identity involve concerns related to self-affirmation,
family acceptance, and acceptance by other homosexuals as well
as the issues specific to parenting and custody. There are other
gay men who told us they had abandoned their gay lifestyle in
order to become a part of the mainstream. These men enter the
heterosexual world, marry, and father children in the hopes of
living a more normal life. Whether or not they are successful in
leaving their sexual attraction to men behind is not documented.

The task of developing a positive gay identity is fraught with
difficulty because gay fathers face rejection by some gay men
who avoid getting involved with a man who is also a father for
fear of the competition that often occurs between the children
and the gay "stepfather" (see chapter 3 for a discussion of this
family type). The gay culture has been built on the basis of men
being single and in short-term relationships. For a man to enter
that social milieu having been involved in a long-term relationship and bring along with him the many commitments of fatherhood (financial, time, and energy) creates an environment with
overtones of discrimination and rejection in both worlds. Many
gay men simply do not want to get into a committed relationship

with a gay father because of competition with his children. Such a marginal existence can cause extreme conflict. One man we talked with entered into a relationship with strong misgivings:

> I suddenly find myself living in the suburbs, driving his kids to school, ball games, and McDonald's. I miss the easy freedom of city life and often find myself resenting the fact that his kids control my life as well as his. It helped when I started spending time in the city with friends on one of the weekend nights he has his kids. That way, they have private time together, and I can get away and enjoy myself. I'm not sure how long this can last, but for now it works because I love him and would rather be with him, even in the suburbs and with his kids.

A growing number of gay men who have lived exclusively homosexual lives are choosing to become parents so they can participate in the experience that comes naturally to their heterosexual brothers. These men may contract with a single woman who either shares custody or gives up her parenting rights. Billy, in talking about his desire to have children, said:

> I had always wanted to be a father, and I really couldn't see why it wouldn't work. Jim and I had been together for twelve years. We mixed our sperm together and a friend of ours was artificially inseminated. We're not sure who Mike's real father is. What's important is that both of us love him and are proud to claim him as a son. He seems to like the idea of having two daddies as well as a mommy.

Oftentimes such shared parenting arrangements bring together a gay male couple and a lesbian couple to serve as parents for their child (see chapter 3).

The reasons that gay men choose to become parents are every bit as diverse as those given by heterosexual men (Robinson & Barret, 1986). The important fact is that these men become parents and strive to create lives that offer security and happiness for their children as well as themselves. It is important to validate the very strong contributions that gay men can make in their fathering roles. Whether with the assistance of a mental health professional or on their own, these men must juggle a number of very complex issues as they integrate the roles that characterize their lives. Unfortunately, when they consult with mental health professionals for assistance, they do not always have a positive experience. Children too often feel caught between two worlds. As Box 1–1 illustrates, Chip sometimes feels that he lives on the fringe.

Box 1–1
CHILDREN LIVING ON THE FRINGE

My name is Chip and I'm seventeen and in twelfth grade. When we first moved to Indianapolis, I learned my dad was gay; I was twelve. I didn't really think much about it. There was a birthday coming up and Dad said we were going to go out and buy a birthday card. He went out, drove around the block, and then parked back in front of our house. Then he took me to the park and told me the facts of life. He asked me if I knew what it meant to be gay. I told him, "Yeah, it means to be happy and enjoy yourself." Then he started to explain to me about being homosexual. I really didn't know what it was at that point, until he explained it to me.

It's an accepted part of my life now. I've been growing up with it for almost ten years. When he invites another guy into the house, it's okay. I don't bring other kids home. One of my friends is extremely homophobic and he lets that fact be known. I wouldn't dare risk anything or it would be like "good-bye" to my friend. My other two friends, I don't know how they would react. So I have to be careful about having certain friends over. To me it's blatantly obvious. Having been exposed to so many gay people, I know what to look for and what I'm seeing. Sometimes it's kind of hard because people make fun of gay people. And if I stick up for their rights, then I get ridiculed. So I just don't say anything at school. It's kind of hard sometimes.

The good thing is that you get a more objective view of people in general, being raised by someone who's so persecuted by society. You begin to sympathize with anyone who is persecuted by society. You tend not to be as prejudiced. You tend to appreciate people for what they are, just personally as opposed to color, religion, or sexual preference. That's the best thing. The hardest thing is hearing all these people making cracks or jokes on TV or at school and not really being able to do anything about it. Because he's my dad after all. It makes me kind of sad. I never feel ashamed or embarrassed, but I do feel a little pressured because of this. One time a friend of mine made a joke about gay people. I just played it off like I thought it was funny, but I didn't. You have to pretend that you think the same thing they do when you don't. That makes me feel like a fraud.

When my dad puts his arm around another man, the first thing I think is, "I could never do that." It makes me a little bit uncomfortable, but I'm not repulsed by it. There are times I wish he wouldn't do it, but other times I'm glad he can have the freedom to do it. When he first came out to me, the only question I asked him was, "What are the chances of me being gay?" He couldn't answer it. But today, to the best of my knowledge, I'm not gay. I like chasing after girls.

Sometimes I feel like I'm keeping a big secret. My dad had a holy union with a man once. My friends had these big plans and we were all going out on the day of this big event. And I couldn't go and couldn't explain why. Things like that have happened a number of times. I can't go and I can't tell why. They start yelling at me and get mad. They'll get over it; it's none of their business.

As fathers go, mine tends to be a little nicer—almost a mother's temperament. A friend of mine's father is strict and almost never acknowledges that he's even there. Another friend's father doesn't spend much time with him. They just seem to have stricter parents than mine. I don't know if that's just because of his personality in general or if it's because he's gay. He's a very emotional person; he cries easily. I love him. He's a good dad. He's more open than other dads. He doesn't let me get away with a lot. He tends to be more worried about me and a girl together than some other fathers are about their sons—more worried about my having sex. Whenever I go out on a date, he always says something like, "Don't do anything I wouldn't do," only he doesn't say it jokingly. Sometimes he's just overly cautious.

If I could change my dad and make him straight, I wouldn't do it. It might make things easier for me in some ways, but I wouldn't have grown up the way I have. Being exposed to the straight world and gay world equally has balanced me out more than some of the other people I know. The only thing I'd want to change is society's treatment of him.

Gay Men in Therapy: An Overview

The history of gay men as consumers of psychotherapy is not altogether pleasant. Experiencing rejection in their personal lives, many gay men also encounter a counselor who has not resolved his or her own homophobic attitudes. As part of his coming out, Bill consulted with four different counselors before he found one who would take his homosexual feelings seriously:

> The first three listened to me for a bit and then said something like, "Oh Bill, you're not a homosexual." Naturally I was relieved to hear that, but in each instance the sexual attraction to men did not go away! So it took me twenty years to finally decide that I was going to get some help with this issue. I realized that the men and women I had approached for help were dealing with their own discomfort about homosexuality and were unable to really hear my issues. Now I am seeing someone who has been quite helpful. He keeps insisting that I am not gay but probably bisexual, and he thought I made a big mistake when I told my kids, but he's the best I can find in this community. It's too bad there are not more openly gay therapists here. That's what I really need.

Bill's comments are not unusual outside of major metropolitan areas. In spite of the fact that an estimated 25 to 65 percent of gay men seek mental health services (a rate two to four times higher than for heterosexuals), satisfaction is low (Bell & Weinberg, 1978; Jay & Young, 1979; Rudolph, 1988). Still, to a certain extent Bill's experience points out the role that homophobia plays for both individuals in the counseling relationship. Perhaps one reason Bill waited so long to come to terms with his sexuality is that he was simply too afraid to face that aspect of himself to present it to a counselor in stronger and more determined terms; it is also possible that a more gay-positive counselor might have helped Bill address these issues much earlier.

In 1973, the American Psychiatric Association (APA) formally redefined homosexuality, removing it from a list of pathologies and stating that it implied "no impairment in judgement, stability, or general social or vocational capabilities" (American

Psychiatric Association, 1974, p. 497). Although rejected by over one-third of APA members, this ruling effectively ended the use of homosexuality as a diagnosable mental illness. However, research studies continue to indicate that the rank and file of psychiatry still hold negative views of homosexuals. Lief (1977) polled 2,500 psychiatrists and found that 69 percent agreed that homosexuality is inherently pathological. On the other hand, Thompson and Fishburn (1977) reported that 53 percent of sixty-four master's and doctoral degree counseling students believed that homosexuality was not a solid basis upon which to evaluate a person's ability to function. Isay (1989) presents the most compelling review of the impact of the APA's change of definition on psychiatry and concludes that the profession still has a long way to go in ridding itself of a damaging homophobia. Rudolph (1988) concludes his review of the literature on this topic:

> The counselor is torn. He or she is formally told one thing about homosexuality from the profession (i.e., "homosexuality is okay"), and more informally, but no less persuasively, quite another from society-at-large ("homosexuality is not okay"). Support for this contention is provided by data indicating attitudes toward homosexuality in the adult population to be generally more consistently (albeit not exclusively) antigay in nature than is true of the attitudes of human service personnel (e.g., Gallup, 1977; National Opinion Research Center, 1985). Unlike human service professionals, those in the general population are not in the untenable position of having to serve two masters (p. 167).

The counselor providing services to gay men often experiences significant conflict around this issue.

Unfortunately, few training programs even address the issue of providing mental health services to gay men and lesbians. As in other mental health issues, the first step in preparation involves an assessment of one's own attitudes about homosexuality. The beginning point in this task calls for the counselor to examine his or her own feelings, thoughts, and fantasies related to same-sex eroticism. Given society's negative attitude toward homosexuality, the mere process of validating same-sex attraction may generate significant anxiety. The professional who is unable to get beyond his or her own fears surrounding homosexual thoughts and feelings should immediately refer the client to another professional who is more gay-positive.

Typically the focus of counseling sessions with gay men and lesbians includes issues related to coming out, the client's own internalized homophobia, and developmental concerns resulting from insufficient socialization to homosexual subcultures. The client who is coming out will experience anxiety around feared rejection from family and friends as well as struggle with learning to prize his or her homosexuality. The successful integration of the homosexual aspects of personality with the client's broader life structure can become an arduous process that involves depression and anxiety as well as joy and relief.

Many homosexuals have been deprived of the socialization process that most adolescents experience during their high school years. There are virtually no positive public models of gay and lesbian relationships on which to build expectations, and there are few gathering places for homosexual teenagers that provide a positive atmosphere for sexual development and intimacy. Many gay men deal with this deprivation by going through a delayed adolescence as part of their coming out process. Their social lives have an atmosphere of intrigue and excitement one would normally associate with early adolescence. Falling in and out of love at the drop of a hat, they may worry excessively about the superficiality of their social network. Over time, these developmental issues will pass as the client undertakes a more complete integration of his or her sexuality into a unique pattern of living.

One barrier to the successful integration of homosexuality is the client's own internalized homophobia. Reporting anger and resentment toward friends and family members who do not readily accept their homosexuality may be a screen to avoid dealing with one's acceptance of oneself. Tom said:

> I would get so angry with my mother. She would write me these awful letters about how I was ruining her life and warning me not to bring my friends to see her. I tried so hard to explain what was happening. I just wanted her to understand. Finally,

one day my counselor said, "Maybe the real problem is your understanding, not hers." Until he said that I had not realized that I was afraid of myself and just projected all of my own fears onto my mother. How could she ever learn to accept me until I learned to do that for myself?

Another client, Henry, said:

I was so angry that my brothers and sisters did not want to know about my new life. When they came to visit me, I took them to a gay restaurant and bar. They made numerous negative comments about men holding hands and dancing together and finally asked me to take them home. I decided I would never have anything to do with them again if they were going to be so critical of the way I live my life.

Eventually Henry learned that he was demanding his family to accept him, but he was unable to accept their somewhat normal discomfort in the homosexual world. Rather than rejoice over the gift they offered in going out with him, he blamed them for what was really his inability to maintain a positive gay identity when faced with negative comments. Such internalized homophobia is typical as gay men and lesbians come out.

There are no studies that report the experiences of gay fathers in therapy. But several investigations about the experiences of gay men and lesbians in the mental health system exist. Beane (1981) suggests that the task is to help the client develop a positive gay identity, a difficult undertaking in a society that is blatantly antigay. Helping the client re-evaluate his personal values relative to homophobic introjections, gay male stereotypes, masculinity, and sexual activity and monogamy are central to the successful outcome of therapy. Providing a safe place for the gay male who is coming out to have contact with himself, to rediscover his body and emotions, and to learn ways of supporting his often tentative positive gay identity are major tasks for the therapist. For many gay clients, the only place where they can discuss their sexuality without encountering society's fear and mistrust may be in the counselor's office. Helping the client find support in the community at large will be an important aspect of the treatment.

Decker (1984) identifies specific issues in counseling gay and lesbian couples. Many times the counselor may be misled into thinking that the problems being presented are grounded in the couple's sexual orientation when, in fact, the distress in these couple relationships can be traced to developmental issues and family dynamics that would cause similar difficulty in a hetero-sexual relationship. About the only thing unique about working with a gay or lesbian couple is the prevalence of boundary-related issues. For example, because our social systems often fail to validate the importance and permanence of the gay or lesbian relationship, the couple can become isolated and alienated from their families of origin and from aspects of the subculture. The tendency is for both members of the couple to expect a relation-ship that is perfect and satisfies every need. Naturally, integrat-ing this relationship into the larger family of origin is a signifi-cant task and one that may never be initiated.

If one or both of the couple have come from an enmeshed family, there may be significant distress over intimacy issues. In short, the relationship may be troubled because of an insufficient amount of external support. The absence of shared children, legal sanction, and the prevailing single lifestyle focus within the gay subculture combine to present serious, and often destruc-tive, obstacles for the gay and lesbian couple. Decker encourages the counselor to spend significant time on family of origin issues, to carefully look for unresolved coming out issues, to be open to the way each couple constructs a unique model of a successful relationship, and to avoid imprinting the heterosexual marriage model on gay men and lesbians.

One gay father, Bill, said:

> When I was nineteen, I went to the most respected psychiatrist in my community and told him I thought I was gay. We talked a few times and he told me, "Don't worry about it. This is just a phase. You are not sick like the queers you see on TV. You will grow out of it." I took his advice, and I started going out with women, married, and found myself a father at age twenty-two. The attraction to men wouldn't go away though, and after a few years I knew I had to be honest with myself. My wife left me when she found out, and I've not been allowed to even see my son since he was five years old. I know where he is now,

and I suppose I could write to him. But I'm sure she has poisoned him against me. I don't think there's any point in my messing up his life now. Maybe if he wants to find me, we will meet one day. I think about him a lot. That damn psychiatrist shares some of the blame for this. If he had just taken me seriously, I would never have married and had a son. I'll never trust a counselor again.

Providing mental-health services to gay fathers is a very complex task. For gay fathers, resolving the grief that accompanies any failed relationship, finding ways to assist in the acquisition of a new support system, and facing the potential rejection by children are the three major counseling issues that must be resolved. The prevalence and complexity of pain in each case can become overwhelming to both the client and the counselor. It is not a task to be undertaken lightly.

Tips for Practitioners

Fortunately, there are some specific guidelines to assist the beginning counselor working with gay men and lesbians. Most clients will be quite patient and understanding of the counselor who has not had experience with homosexual clients. It is important that the counselor present him or herself in a genuine manner by acknowledging a lack of intimate knowledge about a particular culture. The client will be glad to teach the empathic counselor, who can offer a safe place for the exploration of feelings. The following suggestions highlight some of the major issues that can be anticipated.

FOSTER SELF-ACCEPTANCE

When fathers are the primary clients, they often need positive support and encouragement as they reformulate their sexual identities. Usually, this reformulation surfaces through turmoil and anxiety. The conflict can become so severe that suicide attempts may occur. Resolving the conflict is partly a consequence of helping gay fathers accept themselves for who they are and resolving the internalized negative stereotypes of homosexuality.

Self-acceptance is often resolved through disclosure and acceptance by loved ones. Of course, the fear of rejection is always a possibility for which gay fathers must prepare themselves, as a gay father lamented:

> My son is now eleven, and I find myself trying to reinforce the bond of friendship and love between us so that when he understands my sexual orientation, he will be able to draw on the strength of our relationship to weather what I anticipate may well be a difficult time. My greatest fear is that my son will reject me and choose to live apart from me. This is the one fear that I think is unique to being a single gay father. I look forward to the day when this fear is history!

DEAL WITH ONGOING ISSUES THAT RESURFACE

Coming out and developing a positive gay identity are lifelong tasks that may need periodic refinement. The gay and lesbian subculture is exceedingly rich and diverse, and it is probable that people will move through different aspects of it over time. A "phase of life" surrounding bars and other more superficial relationships can mature into a social life revolving around dinner gatherings, theater outings, and other activities that simply reflect the culture of the larger community. Further, it is not uncommon for gay fathers to experience grief over being gay at significant family turning points. For instance, at family gatherings like marriages, family reunions, births, illnesses, or funerals, the client's homosexuality may become an issue that can trigger unresolved self-hatred and fear. Whereas coming out to one's family does communicate the development of a positive gay identity, expecting the client to disclose to his family before he is ready is inappropriate. Some gay men never come out to their families; their right to control who they tell may be the only thing that they feel they do control and must be respected.

PROVIDE NETWORK OPPORTUNITIES

More specialized services are needed to meet the needs of gay men, some of whom are still married, agonizing over divorce and custody issues, and others, still in the process of coming out, who are struggling with identity concerns. Helping gay fathers establish social networks composed of both homosexuals and heterosexuals who accept both identities can help them resolve this conflict. Practitioners can arrange group discussions, even if involving only two gay fathers. Groups allow the men to share their pain, failures, joys, and successes and can be helpful, especially during the rough early days of coming out, resolving identity conflict, and separating from the children's mother. According to Mager (1975), "Such meetings would break down the isolation, would bring the feeling of self-confidence, and would open up alternatives which a person might not think of" (p. 132).

This same process of integrative sanctioning (Bozett; 1981a, 1981b) is evident as the client begins to disclose his gay identity to heterosexuals and his fathering role to other gay individuals. His worst fear may be that he does not belong in either world, creating an overwhelming sense of alienation. Supporting him as he identifies support within the larger community or in nearby communities can help ease this process. Gay father groups that meet in larger metropolitan areas offer a significant affirmation and a place to sort out some of the more pressing issues. Simply corresponding with one of these groups may ease some of the sense of isolation. Talking to other gay fathers and reading the scant literature on gay fathers also can be helpful. Finding gay neighborhoods, gay churches, and legal support organizations will be reassuring to the newly out gay father.

Thoughts of suicide often accompany major life changes that involve loss and being out of control. Many gay fathers express their deep despair by talking about ending their lives. Whereas these threats must be taken seriously, activating an extended support network will do much to ameliorate them. For example, simply being able to refer the client to other gay fathers in your community will provide testimony that will normalize the client's experience and lessen his sense of alienation.

The Gay Father's Coalition can serve as a source of social support for gay men and their families. Contact with other gay fathers through this organization can resolve feelings of isolation and alienation and help in conflict resolution. The Gay Father's Coalition is a group of gay fathers who, despite varied experiences, are united to help each other integrate the two aspects of their lives. The Coalition's overriding belief is that gay men can love and nourish children and provide a safe environment in which their kids can mature into loving and productive men and women. The organization was originally formed to help gay men to grow and develop and to draw upon the rich experiences of both aspects of their lives. This is achieved through mutually supportive groups for building a positive self-image and for creative problem solving. The Coalition locates other gay men who are fathers, are contemplating fatherhood, or may be struggling alone. It also educates professionals and the general public about the special concerns of being a gay parent. The appendix of this book provides the address of the Coalition as well as other organizations that serve as supports for gay men struggling with fatherhood and sexuality issues.

REFRAIN FROM PREMATURE LABELING

The father who has been deeply closeted may prematurely rush to label himself as gay when, in fact, he may actually have more of a bisexual orientation. Such premature labeling and disclosure can create major difficulties, once his life has settled into a more familiar pattern. Cautioning against premature labeling must be done in an atmosphere that is gay-positive. It is essential that the client perceive this "warning" as an expression of concern for his well-being rather than as simply one more homophobic response.

Helping gay fathers work through these issues can be rewarding. As time passes and the family recovers from their initial loss, significant growth can occur. Of course, not all families will completely incorporate their loved one's sexual orientation, but many come to realize that being gay is just one aspect of the person they love, and they find that they have a new relationship based on a stronger awareness of integrity and respect.

References

American Psychiatric Association (1974). Position statement on homosexuality and civil rights. *American Journal of Psychiatry, 131,* 497.
Beane, J. (1981). "I'd rather be dead than gay": Counseling gay men who are coming out. *Personnel and Guidance Journal, 60,* 222–226.

Bell, A. P. & Weinberg, M. S. (1978). *Homosexualities: A Study of Diversity among Men and Women.* New York: Simon & Schuster.

Bozett, F. W. (1981a). Gay fathers: Evolution of the gay father identity. *American Journal of Orthopsychiatry, 51,* 552–559.

Bozett, F. W. (1981b). Gay fathers: Identity conflict resolution through integrative sanctioning. *Alternate Lifestyles, 4,* 90–107.

Bozett, F. W. (1980). Gay fathers: How and why they disclose their homosexuality to their children. *Family Relations: Journal of Applied Family and Child Studies, 29,* 173–179.

Bozett, F. W. (October 16, 1984). "The Children of Gay Fathers: Strategies for Coping with Identity Variance." Paper presented at the National Council on Family Relations, San Francisco, CA.

Decker, B. (1984). Counseling for gay and lesbian couples. *Practice Digest, 7*(1), 13–15.

Fadiman, A. (1983). The double closet. *Life Magazine, 6,* 76–100.

Gallup, G. (1977). *The Gallup Opinion Index (report no. 147).* Princeton, NJ: The American Institute of Public Opinion.

Harry, J. (1983). Gay male and lesbian relationships. In E. D. Macklin & R. H. Rubin (eds.), *Contemporary Families and Alternative Lifestyles.* Beverly Hills, CA: Sage.

Herscher, E. (November 27, 1989). AIDS child with two lesbian moms. *San Francisco Chronicle,* A8.

Hitchens, D. (1980). Social attitudes, legal standards, and personal trauma in child custody cases. *Journal of Homosexuality, 5,* 89–95.

Isay, R. A. (1989). *Being homosexual: Gay Men and Their Development.* New York: Farrar, Straus, Giroux.

Jay, K. & Young, A. (1979). *The Gay Report.* New York: Summit.

Kirk, K. & Madsen, H. (1989). *After the Ball: How America Will Conquer its Fear and Hatred of Gays in the 90s.* New York: Doubleday.

Lief, H. L. (1977). Sexual survey no. 4: Current thinking on homosexuality. *Medical Aspects of Human Sexuality, 11,* 110–111.

Maddox, B. (1982). *Married and Gay.* New York: Harcourt, Brace, and Jovanovich.

Mager, D. (1975). Faggot father. In K. Jay & A. Young (eds.), *After You're Out.* New York: Gage.

Marciano, T. D. (1985). Homosexual marriage and parenthood should not be allowed. In N. H. Feldman & M. Feldman (eds.), *Current Controversies in Marriage and Family.* Beverly Hills, CA: Sage, 293–302.

Miller, B. (1979a). Gay fathers and their children. *The Family Coordinator, 28,* 544–552.

Miller, B. (1979b). Unpromised paternity: Lifestyles of gay fathers. In M. Levine (ed.), *Gay Men: The Sociology of Male Homosexuality.* New York: Harper & Row.

Miller, B. (1978). Adult sexual resocialization. *Alternate Lifestyles, 1,* 207–234.

National Opinion Research Center (1985). *General Social Surveys, 1972–1985: Cumulative Codebook.* Chicago: University of Chicago.

Pleck, J. & Sawyer, J. (1974). Men and children. In J. Pleck & J. Sawyer (eds.), *Men and Masculinity.* Englewood Cliffs, NJ: Prentice-Hall.

Robinson, B. & Barret, R. (1986). Gay fathers. In B. Robinson & R. Barret, *The Developing Father.* New York: Guilford.

Ross, H. L. (1971). Mode of adjustment of married homosexuals. *Social Problems, 18,* 385–393.

Rudolph, J. (1988). Counselor's attitudes toward homosexuality: A review of the literature. *Journal of Counseling and Development, 67,* 165–168.

Thompson, G. J. & Fishburn, W. R. (1977). Attitudes towards homosexuality among graduate counseling students. *Counselor Education and Supervision, 17,* 121–130.

Walters, L. H. & Elam, A. W. (1985). The father and the law. *American Behavioral Scientist, 29,* 78–111.

Weitzman, L. J. & Dixon, R. B. (1979). Child custody awards: Legal standards and empirical patterns for child custody, support, and visitation after divorce. *University of California–Davis Law Review, 12,* 473–521.

Wyers, N. L. (1987). Lesbian and gay spouses and parents: Homosexuality in the family. *Social Work, 32,* 143–148.

2

Gay Fathers
Myths and Realities

I've been married for twenty-seven years. I'm forty-seven years old, and my wife and I have two children, both of whom have left home. When I learned that my wife had been secretly taking valium for seventeen years and was alcohol and valium addicted, it obviously explained a lot of things that had not happened in our relationship. Her recovery has brought to the surface many issues in our marriage, particularly for me a lot of questions about my own sexuality and whether this is a relationship I want to be in for the rest of my life. There are times when I feel attracted to men, although I've never acted on those feelings, even though they've been there for years. It's come along at a time when our children are getting married and leaving home, which also provided another opportunity for me to feel like it's time to make a decision about whether or not I want to be in this relationship for the rest of my life. For the last several years as I've worked with AIDS patients, I've been exposed to more and more gay people and find that there's a lot more variety in the gay culture than I had imagined. The stereotype of the very effeminate, campy gay man is just one kind of gay person. There are other gay men who are very professional who don't relate to the stereotypical culture and don't seem to thrive on that. Their lives are directed toward other activities and building good relationships with people. This discovery has caused me to think, "Well, maybe that could be me." In the past when I'd have these feelings, I'd see gay men and say, "That's not like me. I'm not like them." And now I'm seeing more of these other people who are kind of like me. And I'm thinking, "Well, maybe that *is* me and maybe I *do* belong there and maybe that's where I fit." I guess as I've been struck by all that, I have not felt good about covering up these feelings all these years. There's a part of me that says, "Finally be honest. You've got these years ahead of you. At least be honest in these years and live your life as the person you are."

In some ways being forty-seven encourages me to not do it because I see myself at a time in life when sexuality is less important than it would have been earlier. I see myself, if I find out I am a gay man, with fewer prospects for a partner, because I'm less attractive than I would have been fifteen years ago. I'm less flexible in my ability to learn about the single world, what that's like, and how to move in it. And so that worries me, and I think this is not the time to be doing this. I should have made this change fifteen years ago. But it is an issue of integrity, to a certain extent, to be real, free, and whoever I am.

I realize that a piece of this is a struggle of identity. I got married when I was twenty. I went from the family I grew up in to the marriage, and I've never lived alone. Part of the struggle for me would exist if I were heterosexual or homosexual. It has to do with who I am as a single person and what kind of life I can create for myself as a single person, how I would handle loneliness, who would be my friends, how my children would respond to me as a single person or a gay person. There's so much unknown there. I don't know many single people. It feels a bit like, I get myself out here and I'm going to be alone for life. On the other hand, in terms of belonging, I grew up feeling like I didn't belong in my family. I'm real different from my brothers. It was clear all along that my family was baffled that I was so different from them. I'm different politically, socially, and intellectually. They never could understand that, and that difference was always seen in a negative light because I was not like them. So I grew up feeling like I didn't really belong. During the teenage years, I wasn't athletic. I was a good student and had friends and people I did things with. I worried a lot about what group I belonged to and who liked me for myself. I guess I've felt different from most of the men I've known all these years. I was real interested in my children when they were babies, and I enjoyed taking care of them.

And most of my male friends were not interested in that at all. The kinds of things that young men were supposed to be involved in, like career, golf, and tennis, I could care less about. I was much more interested in talking about books and movies and had very few men I could do that with. So I often felt that I didn't belong over the years. There are times in the gay culture that it seems that here is a group of people who welcome me—and I belong. People I talk to seem happy to claim me as a gay person. I don't know if it's gay pride or what it is. There's a gay movement that is seeking more recognition and legitimacy in the mainstream. I think they're looking for people who can represent them well in the community.

I keep thinking, "If I am a gay person why haven't I acted on it?" There are times I think that if I could be free enough, it would feel so good to have sex with another man—to at least try it. There are other times that it scares me, particularly with the AIDS epidemic. It seems like such a big risk. The freedom that once existed doesn't exist anymore. My wife is the only person I've ever had sex with in my life. It seems like I'm taking steps that I can't come back from and I'm beginning to define myself in a way that is scary. I'm not sure what all the consequences are for me if I am gay. That feels scary and lonely. I cannot envision what a life for me as a gay man would be like. It seems like so many gay lives revolve around gay bars, big social gatherings, and a lot of glitter. And I'm not interested in that. So opportunities to meet gay men and be with gay men seem limited. If I decide that I'm gay and I'm sitting home in my living room, what good is that going to do me? I'll be sitting there by myself until I die. So I have to figure out a way to get into a social system that must exist somewhere. The men in that system are probably ten to fifteen years younger than me and that feels awkward to me. I'm not sure where I'd find men my own age. Being gay is more than just having sex with men. But I'm not sure what all of it does mean.

I would want my children to know that I am gay, if that's a lifestyle I choose. Trying to communicate that to my children in a way that they could understand seems impossible as well as painful. I worry that if I had to do that, they would not want to see me again. They would see me as this perverted person that they don't want to be around or want their children around. At times I wonder who would respect me and if I could respect myself. It's hard for me to figure out how I'll deal with rejection. In terms of being a grandfather or a father, I could do that well and be gay. I think their children would think I'm a little funny, and that would just have to be okay. I don't want to lead two separate lives. I want to have a life where I can be who I am, be free, not hide who I am, and be at peace with myself.

If I had not had kids, I would have made this decision a long time ago. I have put it off because my first daughter was born when I was twenty-three, and this is not something she asked for. I didn't want her to grow up and have to deal with that. I didn't want to deal with it either. Then as the other two children came along, I felt that I had to give them the best they could get and when they're ready to go, I'd figure out what to do next. Being their father and supporting their lives has been very important to me. Now that they're out of the nest, I can think more about what's best for me, not what's best for them. I think my marriage wouldn't have survived if there had not been children because it's been a bad marriage for a long time. The children kept us together. Now that they have moved out, I'm determined it's my time to create a different kind of life and make it what I want for a change. I never had the young adult years of being out in the world because the family had to come first. I just couldn't reconcile my homosexuality and fathering role.

There are times when I feel absolutely sure that I am gay and there's no doubt in my mind. But sometimes it seems that maybe I'm just anxious and just want to get it over with. I believe that sexuality falls on a continuum and that people are at different places. At times it seems much safer to be either heterosexual or gay. That's more manageable than to be somewhere in between. That's the ultimate confusion for me. How do I build a life if I'm somewhere in between? That's real confusing. Most of the time when people say they're bisexual, I always thought that was a cop out and that they were really gay and didn't want to come to terms with it. But maybe I'm wrong. Most of my sexual thoughts right now have to do with men, and I don't feel drawn to sexual relationships with women. I don't even think about women. So I tend to think that I am a gay man. My decision about it is the important thing, and if I decide that too quickly, I may be giving up something that's very important.

Two months ago when I made the decision to do something about my homosexual feelings, I felt real clear that this

was the right thing to do. I felt intense excitement and antici-
pation about being able to create this different kind of life for
myself and being free of the bad feelings that have come with
sexual attraction for men. I felt almost drawn to embrace this
part of me that I have tried to push away. And that felt wonderful! At the same time, I was scared about whether people
would accept me and if there would be people whom I would
have relationships with. But I finally decided that that's not the
issue. The important thing is having integrity about who I am
as a person. As I've gotten closer to the point of separating
from my wife, this tremendous fear has taken over. All that
certainty and excitement very rarely break through. There's
nothing to carry me forward at this point. I'm immobilized by
fear. There's also a sense of urgency at times, feeling like life
is hanging in the balance. Sometimes I wonder if we should
address the issues between us or put them off until I get this
other part of me straightened out. And I feel like I'm not being
fair to my wife, yet staying doesn't feel fair to me. Sometimes
I wonder if I think the grass is greener on the other side. I fear
that I'll get on the other side and carry all these feelings with
me that I don't belong, and I won't have any of the social support that I have on this side. I was thinking last Sunday in
church, "Do I really believe God can respect me as a gay person?" The message that day was that "marriage is forever,"
that two people become one and that union lasts forever.

I was of course, troubled by that because that was the day
after I had decided I would leave my wife. I also wondered if
there was a special meaning in the message for me. Along with
that I began to wonder who would respect me as a gay person.
A lot of people would not respect me. That's all they would see.
Who I am as a person wouldn't matter nearly as much as who
I am as a *gay* person. Of course, the key is that I must respect
myself, and if I do that, the rest of it will take care of itself.
That's what I'm trying to figure out now. How do I do that? It
feels like there's a lot of pain ahead.

By January 1989, Colin had moved into an apartment of his
own, and he and his wife of twenty-seven years had started legal
separation proceedings. By the spring of 1990, he had moved
three thousand miles away from his family and was living in an
all-gay community. Colin left the heterosexual world where he

had spent a lifetime and entered the gay world where, the last time we talked to him, he had established a solid network of new gay friends. Much of the information in this book is based on ten years of research and personal interviews with gay fathers. The pain and anguish of coming to terms with the incompatibility of being a father (a heterosexual role) and a gay man (a homosexual role) are illustrated in our conversation with Colin.

Myths and Research

Throughout this book, we will document scientific findings, our own as well as others, with anecdotal material that we have collected from gay fathers over the years. In our studies we discovered numerous myths that are generally held about these men. Noted anthropologist Ashley Montagu (1978) believes such myths derive from stereotypes and misinformation: "Homosexuality is not a problem that homosexuals create, but one that ill-informed and bigoted people create whose emotional conflicts about their own sexual difficulties they frequently tend to project upon others" (p. 91). The myths that we have found include the following:

Disturbed Parental Relationships Myth. Homosexuals, including gay fathers, have disturbed parental relationships (i.e., cold, rejecting fathers and emotionally smothering mothers) that cause them to become attracted to same-sex partners.

Macho Myth. Gay fathers, capable of having sex with a female, are more masculine than gay men in general.

Germ Myth. Interactions between gay fathers and their children will lead to transmission of homosexuality to their offspring. Children of homosexual fathers will turn out to be homosexual themselves.

Harassment Exposure Myth. Gay fathers expose their children to harassment and embarrassment because of societal disapproval.

Molestation Myth. There is a high incidence of sexual abuse among children of gay fathers. Gay men in general and gay fathers in particular sexually exploit unsuspecting children.

Sex Fiend Myth. The main goal in life for gay fathers is primarily that of sexual gratification.

Smoke Screen Myth. Gay men become fathers as a cover to hide their homosexuality so they can function more easily in society.

Compensation Myth. Gay men enter into heterosexual relationships and have children to compensate for and deny their homosexual feelings.

Identification Myth. Homosexual men marry and become fathers in order to identify with the feelings and the feminine roles of their wives.

Sick Myth. Gay fathers are psychologically sick and need therapy to help them change their sexual orientation so that it is more compatible with their fathering role.

Many of these myths emerged because there have been so few scientific studies conducted on gay fathers. During the 1970s, as researchers began to realize the important roles fathers play in their children's development, and with the advent of changing sex roles and a greater acceptance of homosexuality among professional organizations, "the age of gay parenthood" emerged from the closet. The information unearthed from these studies debunks each of the preceding myths about gay fathers and helps us gain a better understanding of their plight than professionals have held in the past.

Our main theme throughout our research on homosexuality and the family has been the nature of the relationships between gay fathers and their families and friends. Our interest in this subject began with a national study on gay men's and women's perceptions of their early family life and how they saw their relationships with parents (see box 2–1). Our positive findings refuted the stereotype of a sick family history as a necessary condition for homosexuality to occur. This caused us to question

Box 2–1
A NATIONAL STUDY

A national study was launched in 1980 as one of the first studies of gay men and lesbian women covering the entire United States (Robinson, Skeen, Flake-Hobson & Herrman, 1982). In order to locate as diverse a sample as possible, the population drew from five regions of the country: 25 percent from the Northeast; 15 percent from the Midwest; 33 percent from the South, 18 percent from the Southwest; and 9 percent from the West. All seventy-two chapters of Dignity, an organization composed of gay men and lesbian women from all denominations and religious preferences, were contacted. Dignity's purpose is to work for the support and acceptance of gay men and women and to elicit responsive approaches from society as a whole.

The questionnaire, designed by us, consisted of three sections. The first section included demographic information. The second section assessed current relationship status and asked respondents to answer "yes" or "no" to such questions as, "Are you currently living with someone? Yes (roommate), yes (lover, opposite sex), yes (lover, same sex) or no." Other questions concerned having previously lived with someone, marital status, and children. The third and main section of the questionnaire contained thirteen items. Five of them measured respondents' perceptions of their mothers' acceptance (Mother Acceptance Scale) and five measured perceptions of their fathers' acceptance (Father Acceptance Scale). Items included acceptance of child's being homosexual, description of relationship with parent, felt loved by parent, ability to live up to parent's expectations, and how parent would rate respondent's worthiness as a child. Respondents were asked to react to questions such as, "How would you describe your relationship with your mother?" with Likert-scale responses (on a scale from 1 to 5, extremely unsatisfactory to extremely satisfactory). Three additional items dealt with family atmosphere during childhood. On a five-point scale, respondents rated degree of marital discord during their upbringing and degree of pleasantness of their childhood until and during adolescence. They were asked if both parents were present in the house during their upbringing, and if not, which parent was absent.

Questionnaires were mailed to all Dignity chapters across the United States that had previously expressed a willingness to participate. Each group leader, who had been given instructions for completing the forms during a regular meeting, distributed questionnaires. The total number of returned forms was 332 (285 men and 47 women), a return rate of 62 percent.

Findings revealed that two-thirds of the sample perceived their relationships with their fathers as extremely satisfactory or satisfactory. Over three-fourths perceived their relationships with their mothers as extremely satisfactory or satisfactory. The majority perceived that both their fathers and mothers would accept their homosexuality. Although relationships with mothers were perceived to be slightly better than relationships with fathers, both maternal and paternal parent-child relationships were described more as adequate and positive than inadequate or negative. In years to come, we will extend this research to include a special focus on gay fathers and a second national study of the parents of gay men and lesbian women (see chapter 5).

---

many of the other myths that surround homosexuality and to examine the gay father's role more closely.

DISTURBED PARENTAL RELATIONSHIPS MYTH

We were particularly interested in understanding the disturbed parental relationship myth surrounding gay fathers and their early parental interactions. The intriguing findings from the national homosexual population compelled us to go a step further and analyze a subsample of responses from gay fathers in the study (Skeen & Robinson, 1984). This turned out to be thirty men, or approximately 10 percent of the sample, who had fathered one or more children. Children of gay fathers ranged in age from one to thirty-four years. The fathers represented five regions of the country: 13 percent Northeast; 23 percent Midwest; 23 percent South; 27 percent Southwest; and 13 percent West. All but one father had at one time been involved in a heterosexual marriage. The profile of early family backgrounds of gay fathers emerging from the data were generally positive. It was not possible to determine from this study what effect (if any) the positive early family experiences had on gay fathers' decisions to become involved in a heterosexual marriage and to father children, since no questions dealt with this issue. But most gay fathers grew up in intact homes where heterosexual relationships were modeled for them, where pleasant memories existed, and where marital discord was uncommon. Although relationships with mothers were perceived to be slightly better than those with fathers, both maternal and paternal parent-child relationships were described more as adequate and positive than inadequate and negative. Most gay fathers also believed that both their mothers and fathers viewed them as worthy individuals, although mothers did so slightly more than fathers. Overall, the findings refuted the old Freudian myths that disturbed parental relationships are necessary and sufficient conditions for gay fathers. In fact, gay fathers seemed to value stability of family relationships from childhood into their adult lives. Asked, "What important things do you want to accomplish in your lifetime?", responses dealt with stabilizing family relationships (50 percent), having a successful career (33 percent), and improving the lot of homosexuals in general (17 percent). One father responded: "Wisdom to tell my children (at the right age) what loving another man means to me—emotionally, mentally, spiritually, but not necessarily physically." Asked, "What thing or things are most important to you in your life right now?", recurrent themes were children, lovers, careers, religion, peace of mind, and health. Many fathers listed both their children and lovers as important. Typical responses were these: "my two children, a new male friend"; "son, job, relationship"; 'building my relationship with my daughter, parents, and lover"; "my children, parents, and church"; "family, friends, my son, and career"; "wife, child, career"; "being more accepted by my children." Practically all fathers had dissolved their heterosexual marriages in favor of homosexual relationships, and many fathers listed both their children and lovers as important in their lives.

To carry the data analysis a step further, a matched sample of gay nonfathers was compared with gay fathers, with particu-

Table 2–1
Summary of Demographic Data on Gay Fathers and Gay Nonfathers

	Gay Fathers (N = 30)			Gay Nonfathers (N = 30)		
	Range 22–62 years	Mean 41.4 years		Range 22–62 years	Mean 41.6 years	
e	White 27	Hispanic 2	Black 1	White 30	Hispanic 0	Black 0
cation	Range 10–22 years	Mean 16.5 years		Range 12–24 years	Mean 16.9 years	
gion	No Preference 2	Catholic 17		No Preference 2	Catholic 21	
	Protestant 10	Jewish 1		Protestant 7	Jewish 0	
me	Range $4,000– $50,000	Median $17,500	Mean $19,550	Range $3,000– 50,000	Median $14,000	Mean $14,117

lar emphasis on parent-son relationships (Skeen & Robinson, 1985). Table 2–1 presents additional demographic information. No difference was found between gay fathers' and gay nonfathers' perceptions of their parents' acceptance of them. Both groups perceived their mothers to be more accepting than their fathers. The majority of gay fathers (24/30) and nonfathers (23/30) had grown up in intact families with both mother and father present. Asked about the presence of marital discord between their parents as they were growing up, an identical number (20) of gay fathers and nonfathers said there was "not a lot." Overall, both gay fathers (25/30) and nonfathers (27/30) rated their childhoods as pleasant rather than unpleasant.

These findings do not support the Freudian-based hypothesis that gay fathers view their early family life and relationships with their fathers and mothers as more positive than gay nonfathers. Instead, no difference was found. Contrary to the Freudian-based hypothesis that homosexuals' families are characterized by negative relationships and abnormality, the majority of both gay fathers and nonfathers grew up in intact homes without much marital discord and viewed their family of orientation as primarily pleasant.

The finding that gay fathers and nonfathers both view their

mothers as more accepting than their fathers is interesting. It could be construed to support the Freudian idea that homosexuals' relationships with their fathers are unsatisfactory, characterized by coldness, rejection, and absence, whereas homosexuals are overly close to their mothers. However, because most of the sample viewed their relationship with their fathers as primarily positive, this explanation seems implausible. A more reasonable explanation may be related to child-rearing practices in general. The men in this sample were likely to have grown up in homes with traditional upbringings in which mothers were the primary caretakers and fathers the economic providers. As a result of these different parenting patterns, heterosexual as well as homosexual children are more likely to feel closer to (that is, more loved, accepted, and valued by) their mothers than their fathers. Taken together, these findings do not support the Freudian-based concept of a causal relationship between early family relationship patterns and sexual orientation. Instead, they support the growing body of research that questions a direct link between early family relationship patterns and sexual orientation.

MACHO MYTH

Traditionally, our society has perpetuated the stereotype that homosexual men are more feminine than heterosexual men and that lesbian women are more masculine than heterosexual women. This stereotype has been refuted by numerous studies that show masculinity and femininity among homosexuals to be unrelated to their sexual lifestyles and that the stereotype of cross-gender endorsement is unfounded (Storms, 1980). Just as femininity and male homosexuality have been connected, there has also been a tendency to link two other unrelated phenomena: masculinity and fatherhood. Here is how a gay father expressed his perception of this myth:

> Being a father and gay man are incompatible. That stems from the notion that gay men are not able to have sex with women so they don't reproduce. Here I suddenly am as a father and

that automatically means I must not be gay. There was a piece of that when I got married. It was sort of like when my wife got pregnant the first time, I thought, "Well, I *am* a man, and I'm not gay." If you can propagate, you're masculine. You're not "weird" or gay.

The macho myth implies that gay fathers, because they marry, have sexual intercourse with the opposite sex, and father children, are more masculine than gay men who do not enter into these relationships. This belief was put to the test by comparing two groups of gay fathers and nonfathers on sex-role orientation (Robinson & Skeen, 1982). The Bem Sex Role Inventory (Bem, 1974) was administered to all participants in the national study, along with the questionnaire. Findings did not support the myth that gay fathers are any more masculine than gay men who do not father children. As table 2–2 shows, a pattern of diverse sex-role orientation was found in which gay men scored equally often masculine, feminine, androgynous (blending both masculine and feminine traits), and undifferentiated, regardless of whether or not they had fathered children. The results indicated that gay fathers and gay nonfathers as a group can be described as more nonandrogynous (that is, either masculine, feminine, or undifferentiated) than androgynous, although fewer fathers scored masculine than in any other category. This finding debunks the myth that masculinity is a prerequisite for fatherhood among gay men and suggests that sexual behavior and sex-role orientation are unrelated phenomena that develop out of separate experiences.

Table 2–2
Frequencies of Gay Men Who Scored Androgynous,
Masculine, Feminine, or Undifferentiated

	Androgynous	*Masculine*	*Feminine*	*Undiffer.*	*Total*
Fathers	9	5	8	8	30
Nonfathers	7	8	6	9	30
Totals	16	13	14	17	60

GERM MYTH

Perhaps the biggest misunderstanding about gay fathers is that they will transmit their homosexuality, deliberately or inadvertently, to their children. The germ myth is related to *homophobia*—an emotional reaction of deep-seated revulsion and fear toward homosexuals and their lifestyles (Weinberg, 1972). The stereotype that general exposure to a gay person will cause one to become homosexual has been generalized from the homosexual population at large to gay fathers and their offspring. A social worker, employed in specialized care for behaviorally and emotionally disabled children, reported common homophobic reactions from the staff:

> A lot of helping professionals, especially men, are afraid that a gay father will seduce them, recruit them, or make some pass at them. They're afraid they're going to catch homosexuality. They don't understand it and think that contact with a gay man will dirty or soil them in some way. Even before the AIDS epidemic, I observed the staff's fear of being contaminated by homosexuals. One staff member said of a gay father in a psychiatric hospital where I worked, "The dad is coming to visit this weekend. I'm glad you're working this weekend and not me." It was like a hot potato that nobody wanted to handle. Recently after an AIDS seminar at our facility, the secretary came in and cleaned her office with Clorox. Although nobody had been there with AIDS, the topic so scared her as a result of the seminar that she was not going to take any chances.

The truth is that most children of homosexual men and women turn out to be heterosexual. Only about 10 percent of the offspring develop homosexual identities, and this figure is proportionate to the number of homosexuals in the population at large. Our own research with 702 parents of homosexual men and women indicates that 90 percent of the parents are heterosexual, 4 percent bisexual, and only 6 percent completely homosexual (Robinson, Walters & Skeen, 1989). One father we spoke with said, "My parents are heterosexual, but I turned out to be gay. So why would anyone believe my homosexuality would rub off on my son?" Another father told us,

I don't believe that if I have questions about myself that my son or daughter will have questions about themselves. I certainly didn't question my sexuality because my father or brother questioned theirs. If they did, I never knew it. I can't see anywhere in my family where anyone else is gay. Nobody has ever approached me sexually or molested me. Never, ever, has anything like that happened to me, and yet I have these feelings. So I don't believe there's any contamination going on. I am whatever I am for whatever reasons I will never know.

Brian Miller (1979) assessed the sexual orientation of the twenty-seven daughters and twenty-one sons of forty gay fathers from cities across the United States and Canada. All the fathers were white, mostly middle class and college-educated, and they ranged in age from twenty-four to sixty-four. According to the fathers' reports, only 8 percent of the children were gay (one of the sons and three of the daughters). Although Miller's study was not randomized, second-generation homosexuals were rare in this sample. Psychiatrist Richard Green (1978) studied thirty-seven children, ranging in age from three to twenty, who were being raised by female homosexuals or by male and female parents who had sex-change surgery. After two years of study, thirty-six out of the thirty-seven children showed clear heterosexual preferences or were developing them. Thirteen adolescent children were attracted to the opposite sex. Green concluded that "The children I interviewed were able to comprehend and verbalize the atypical nature of their parent's lifestyles and to view their atypicality in the broader perspective of the cultural norm" (p. 696). Thus, the homophobic myth that children will be contaminated by their gay fathers is unfounded. A study by the Kinsey Institute of Sex Research, in fact, concluded from a sample of 1,000 homosexuals and 500 heterosexuals that sexual preference results from many factors but begins with an early, probably biological, tendency toward homosexuality or heterosexuality (Bell, Weinberg & Hammersmith, 1981).

HARASSMENT EXPOSURE MYTH

The harassment myth holds that gay fathers expose their children to ridicule and embarrassment because they place their sex-

ual desires above the welfare of their kids. There is an element
of truth to this myth. When gay fathers are open about their
sexuality, their children sometimes face harassment from peers
and other adults. Research, however, shows that gay fathers are
sensitive to the accompanying problems of being the child of a
gay parent. In cases where fathers openly live a homosexual lifestyle, the men ordinarily prepare their children early to deal with
ridicule or they take extra precautions to protect their kids from
harassment (Bozett, 1980). The case of Colin shows how one father suppressed his homosexual identity for twenty years to prevent any emotional harm to his daughters. Other gay fathers
help their children deal with harassment by teaching them about
tolerance of others. There is a tendency for gay fathers to instill
in their children at an early age accepting and nonjudgmental
attitudes toward all human beings, regardless of race, religious
beliefs, or sexual orientation. "If Eryn is gay, he should, unlike
his father, have healthy gay role models to preserve him from
self-hatred and isolation," says one gay father about his son, "If
he is straight, he should have learned tolerance of sexual varia-
tion" (Fadiman, 1983, p. 80).

MOLESTATION MYTH

The molestation myth suggests that gay fathers, because of their
same-sex attraction, will molest their sons or other children. It
further implies that their same-sex preferences are the primary
motivating factors in their lives. A social worker told us that
there happened to be a sex offender on the unit of the psychiatric hospital where she worked. At the same time, a child had
been admitted for chemical dependency. The child's father was
gay, and the staff equated the gay father with the sex offender
who had molested a child. Although this is a common association, the research and statistical data strongly show that this belief is wrong. According to national police statistics, sexual abuse
of children is a heterosexual crime in 90 percent of the cases
(Voeller & Walters, 1978). Social science research also indicates
that sexual exploitation of children by their homosexual parents
is virtually nonexistent (Miller, 1979). One study concludes that,
"the adult heterosexual male constitutes a greater sexual risk to

underage children than does the adult homosexual male" (Groth & Birnbaum, 1978, p. 181).

Sex Fiend Myth

A pervasive myth about gay fathers and homosexuals in general is that sex is all they think about and do. Their sexual preference governs their lives, and they are slaves to their uncontrollable sexual urges. What is not understood is that gay men engage in sexual activity equally as often as their heterosexual counterparts. Being gay refers to a whole approach to life, of which being sexually intimate is one small part. Gay men are viewed suspiciously around children, but especially around boys. Gay men are perceived as having fleeting and superficial relationships and being incapable of committed relationships. Generalized to gay fathers, the sex fiend myth was described by a father struggling with his own sexual identity:

> There is this widespread notion that gay men cannot sustain relationships and tend to be very self-centered. Most of their relationships are fleeting and troubled. The ability to have a positive relationship as a parent would seem to contradict that myth. The notion of a gay man sacrificing his own immediate pleasure for his children sounds contradictory because sexuality is viewed as the prime motivator for gay men. Part of it too is a general belief that gay men would expose their kids to a lot of open sex and are sexually promiscuous and not concerned about how their children view that. If one accepted that myth, then the notion of being committed as a father and being willing to sacrifice as a father would seem unusual.

Smoke Screen Myth

The moving case of Colin in itself is convincing evidence that the incompatibility of being both father and homosexual is not a conscious, deceitful act. Still, this popular belief haunts him.

> I worry that when I tell my old friends that I'm gay they'll respect me less and say, "Well, you're a person who has lived a lie all these years. How dare you come to me for support when all

these years you've been hiding?" That hasn't happened yet.
The people I've talked to have been very accepting and willing
to let me just be where I am.

The smoke screen myth holds that gay men use their marriages and children to conceal their true sexual orientation and
to gain society's acceptance. A newspaper article entitled, "America's Becoming Single-Minded" by Beth Krier (1988) implied
that the smoke screen myth is a common phenomenon—so
common that its discard was offered as one reason for the
rise in single adults: "Some experts suspect that, as society becomes more accepting of alternative lifestyles, fewer homosexuals feel the need to marry to hide their sexual orientation"
(p. 6D).

Research indicates, however, that most gay men enter into
heterosexual relationships and fatherhood with an honest and
authentic desire for successful family relationships and not out
of a desire to mask their homosexuality. Recent data comparing
gay and straight fathers' attitudes and motivations for fatherhood reveal that in both groups marriages and family orientations reflect a traditional attitude toward family life (Bigner &
Jacobsen, 1989). Another study of thirty-two gay fathers found
three major reasons why these men married. In descending order the reasons were: (1) love of prospective spouse; (2) per-
sonal/social expectations; (3) hope that marriage would rid
them of their homosexuality (Wyers, 1987). Although the
majority of gay fathers (68.6 percent) in that study knew
or suspected they were homosexual at or before marriage, many
men do not fully discover their homosexuality until after they
marry.

Other research shows that at the time of marriage many fathers like Colin do not think of themselves as homosexual
(Miller, 1979). Even those fathers who had already had sex with
other men before marriage considered themselves as heterosexual or bisexual. They entered marriage with a genuine love for
their wives and a desire to have children. During the course of
their marriages, they report a conflict between the duality of fatherhood and homosexual awakenings that eventually leads to
an exclusively homosexual orientation (Dank, 1972; Miller,
1978).

COMPENSATION MYTH

This misconception is also widely held by people in general. A common prescription for the "ills of homosexuality" is "a good lay" with a woman. Heterosexual sex and having kids, so it is widely believed, will compensate for the homosexual feelings and thus "cure" gay men. A gay father of two children debunked that myth:

> I had some of the greatest sex you can have with a woman. I was twenty-one dating a woman who was thirty-one. We'd go to bed on Friday and not get up until Sunday afternoon. As far as sex goes, it was great! But as far as the emotional needs and feeling "that something you can only get from another man if you're gay" wasn't there. But coming from a heterosexual background, I thought, "Well I guess this is what it's all about. This is the way it's supposed to be."

IDENTIFICATION MYTH

Another myth that stemmed from the psychoanalytic and unconscious motives for explaining why a homosexual man married and had children was his burning desire to identify with his wife's feminine role. The following passage was presented in a psychiatric journal on a discussion of unmarried fathers:

> After convincing the woman she should marry him, the man turned against her and treated her and the child very sadistically. In all such cases there is some evidence that strong latent homosexual feelings exist in which the good relationship depends upon how much participation the man is permitted in the feelings of the woman. If these are such that he desires vicarious homosexual satisfaction in fantasies, by participating with her in her past life, the situation may be very tolerable. If this does not work out because of too much excitation, the man ends up leaving the woman or treating her miserably (Reider, 1948, p. 234).

SICK MYTH

There is still a pervasive attitude in today's society that recognizes homosexuals and gay fathers as sick and in need of treatment. Pioneer psychoanalytic studies of the 1960s characterized homosexuals, particularly married gay men, as pathological (e.g., Bieber, 1962, 1969). These early studies, riddled with methodological problems and investigator bias, have been severely criticized (Hooker, 1969). Bieber (1962), for example, studied male adult homosexuals and heterosexuals under psychiatric examination for various problems. Not surprisingly, he found pathological themes in his subjects, since they were already under treatment. Bieber's study was further questioned because when analysts were called on to furnish information regarding the data, they knew in which category the patient fell (e.g., either homosexual or heterosexual), thus biasing the observer's opinions and contaminating research results.

These early studies that judged homosexuals to be sick prescribed a changed sexual orientation as a "cure." Today the medical, political, familial, and legal views are more tolerant of gay rights and lifestyles, rather than requiring gay men to change them. More research and gay political clout have contributed a better understanding of homosexuality and changes in the attitudes of political groups as well as professional mental health organizations. In 1973, the American Psychiatric Association voted to no longer classify homosexuality as a mental disturbance, disease, or psychiatric disorder. In 1974, the American Psychological Association removed homosexuality from its Diagnostic and Statistical Manual as a form of mental illness.

Tips for Practitioners

The literature suggests that practitioners have paid little attention to the needs of homosexuals in general and to gay parents in particular. Homophobia pervades the very professions that are committed to helping fellow human beings. Homophobia has been observed among social workers, psychiatrists, and psychologists (Dulaney & Kelly, 1982). Lack of awareness and homophobic attitudes are obstacles to treatment and frequently circumvent gay-father families from seeking treatment altogether. The legal system as well as social service agencies continue to operate and deliver services based on myth and stereotype.

EXAMINE YOUR PREJUDICES

Practitioners must examine their own homophobic prejudices toward homosexuality and gay fathering. Where biases exist, helping professionals can acknowledge and confront them. Recognizing uncomfortable feelings can be a valuable lesson and can be dealt with by gaining more information about gay marriages and lifestyles so that prejudices can be erased. A practitioner told us: "Professionals need more training to better understand what the gay lifestyle is all about. They cling to a lot of myths—like the child molester myth or "a good lay will solve your problems"—that get in the way of the real problems and do more harm than good." It is important for service providers to familiarize themselves with such issues as coming out, divorce, parenting problems, discrimination, and child custody. This can be done in individual counseling or through participation in psychoeducational groups. Learning to identify ways sexual attraction will influence the counseling relationship, developing a sensitivity to the often subtle discriminations that are communicated through language, as well as acquiring information about the subculture, will enable the counselor to get started much more confidently. It is not sufficient to know a few gay men and lesbians; a more systematic approach to raising awareness is necessary.

Talks with married gay men with whom you can make contact or discussions with colleagues who have had experiences working with homosexual couples or married gay men can help. Visits to gay bars, churches, or gay support organizations can be especially valuable. Many organizations also provide speakers for classrooms, churches, or professional organizations. Practitioners can draw upon the resource list and comprehensive bibliography in the Appendix for enlightenment purposes. Additional professional organizations established to prohibit discrimination toward clients on the basis of sexual orientation are also listed in the Appendix of this book. Workers can use this section as a resource bank for gay clients who have accepted their sexuality and wish to meet others to share their interests and concerns. An enlightened response from service providers would be of great value to gay fathers as they attempt to solve the pain and emotional upheaval in their marriages (Wyers, 1987). More enlightened responses are also needed from organizations offering specialized gay and lesbian services that still do not understand or address the unique needs of gay father families. In situations where helping practitioners (whether gay or straight) cannot resolve their prejudices, they should withdraw from the helping role when gay father clients and their families are involved.

USE APPROPRIATE TERMINOLOGY

The parents of a gay son were horrified when their counselor referred to their son's homosexuality as "being that way" and for two sessions not once used the term "gay" or "homosexual." As it turned out, the counselor was afraid the parents were not familiar with the term "gay child" and avoided it for fear of offending them when, in fact, she ended up offending them anyway for not using proper words.

Learning to use appropriate language is just one step in creating the successful therapeutic environment. Make sure you know and use contemporary terms when working with gay parents. The term "gay" is generally preferred to that of "homosexual." Whereas the term "gay" often communicates an attitude of positive self-acceptance, referring to "gays" as a group is generally viewed negatively. Homosexual women often prefer to be referred to as "lesbian."

CLARIFY AND VALIDATE THE CLIENT'S REALITY

It is critical that practitioners help fathers clarify and validate their realities when they confess confused or blurred sexual identity, rather than trying to convince them otherwise. Colin said he tried to address his conflicting homosexual feelings with three different therapists—all of whom denied the possibility of his being homosexual since he was a father. As a result of having his reality invalidated, Colin further buried his feelings and did not deal with them until twenty years later:

> Last week I passed by a construction site and a man was pouring concrete. He had a beautiful body. He had on nothing but jeans and shoes, that was it. I had this strong sexual feeling toward him. I have had those feelings consistently in my life,

but I had not looked at them very hard. But I've wondered what they meant. I've worried about these feelings, but was afraid to talk about them. I tried three times in therapy to talk about my homosexual feelings. The male therapist I was with each time said, "You're not a homosexual." I don't know if they were saying that because they were afraid to talk about it or not. But as each of them said that to me, there was a part of me that wanted to hear it, and I felt a sense of relief, even though I didn't really believe it. Now, twenty years later, I cannot push the feelings aside any longer. I would bring up my homosexuality in therapy because it felt like something that wouldn't go away. But I'm not sure I brought it up with any intention of acting on it. I mostly brought it up hoping I could find a way to forget about it. So I have been afraid of these feelings, and that's what stopped me from doing anything about them. But I have also let that fear dominate me because I was committed to providing this model of a family.

Miller (1979) also reported that a few of the men he interviewed were concerned enough about their homosexual feelings to seek counseling before entering a marital relationship. In each case the man was led to believe that a heterosexual marriage and parenthood would "cure all his ills." In fact, when one of the men fathered a child premaritally, the psychiatrist underscored this as proof that the man was "genuinely heterosexual." A second respondent told of his eagerness to accept his counselor's assessments:

The shrink told me what I was dying to hear: "A person as nice as you couldn't be homosexual." What he should have done was get me to accept my homosexual self rather than some imaginary heterosexual self. But I believed him because I desperately wanted a home and someone to love to come home to (Miller, 1979, p. 546).

References

Bell, A. P., Weinberg, M. S. & Hammersmith, S. K. (1981). *Sexual Preference: Its Development in Men and Women*. Bloomington: Indiana University Press.
Bem, S. L. (1974). The measurement of psychological androgyny. *Journal of Consulting and Clinical Psychology, 42,* 155–162.

Bieber, I. (1969). The married male homosexual. *Medical Aspects of Human Sexuality, 3,* 76–84.

Bieber, I. (1962). *Homosexuality: A Psychoanalytic Study.* New York: Basic Books.

Bigner, J. & Jacobsen, R. (1989). The value of children to gay and heterosexual fathers. *Journal of Homosexuality, 18,* 167–172.

Bozett, F. W. (1980). Gay fathers: How and why they disclose their homosexuality to their children. *Family Relations: Journal of Applied Family and Child Studies, 29,* 173–179.

Dank, B. M. (1972). Coming out in the gay world. *Psychiatry, 34,* 180–197.

Dulaney, D. D. & Kelly, J. (1982). Improving services to gay and lesbian clients. *Social Work, 27,* 178–183.

Fadiman, A. (1983). The double closet. *Life Magazine, 6,* 76–100.

Green, R. (1978). Sexual identity of 37 children raised by homosexual or transsexual parents. *American Journal of Psychiatry, 135,* 692–697.

Groth, N. & Birnbaum, J. (1978). Adult sexual orientation and attraction to underage persons. *Archives of Sexual Behavior, 7,* 175–181.

Hooker, E. (1969). Parental relations and male homosexuality in patient and nonpatient samples. *Journal of Consulting and Clinical Psychology, 33,* 140–142.

Krier, B. (November 7, 1988). "America's Becoming Single-Minded." *The Charlotte Observer,* 6D.

Miller, B. (1979). Gay fathers and their children. *The Family Coordinator, 28,* 544–552.

Miller, B. (1978). Adult sexual resocialization. *Alternate Lifestyles, 1,* 207–234.

Montagu, A. (1978, August). A Kinsey report on homosexualities. *Psychology Today,* 62–66, 91.

Reider, N. (1948). The unmarried father. *American Journal of Orthopsychiatry, 18,* 230–237.

Robinson, B. E. & Skeen, P. (1982). Sex-role orientation of gay fathers versus gay nonfathers. *Perceptual and Motor Skills, 55,* 1055–1059.

Robinson, B. E., Skeen, P., Flake-Hobson, C. & Herrman, M. (1982). Gay men's and women's perceptions of early family life and their relationships with parents. *Family Relations, 31,* 79–83.

Robinson, B. E., Walters, L. & Skeen, P. (1989). Response of parents to learning that their child is homosexual and concern over AIDS: A national study. *Journal of Homosexuality, 18,* 59–80.

Skeen, P. & Robinson, B. E. (1985). Gay fathers' and gay nonfathers' relationship with their parents. *The Journal of Sex Research, 21,* 86–91.

Skeen, P. & Robinson, B. E. (1984). Family backgrounds of gay fathers: A descriptive study. *Psychological Reports, 54,* 999–1005.

Storms, M. (1980). Theories of sexual orientation. *Journal of Personality and Social Psychology, 38,* 783–792.

Voeller, B. & Walters, J. (1978). Gay fathers. *The Family Coordinator, 27,* 149–157.

Weinberg, G. (1972). *Society and the Healthy Homosexual.* New York: Doubleday.

Wyers, N. L. (1987). Lesbian and gay spouses and parents: Homosexuality in the family. *Social Work, 32,* 143–148.

3

The Many Faces of Gay Fatherhood

THE CASE OF ANDREW

I'm twenty-eight years old and have been married four and one-half years. I have a daughter three and a son nineteen months. My wife is a registered nurse. I told her about a year ago that I was gay. She was shocked beyond disbelief at first. She was hurt that I hadn't told her when I first acknowledged it in myself. I had toyed with the idea, looked at the issues, and put them on the back burner for years. I was very sexually active with lots of different women in high school and college. I was a very typical American male. I played football, I swam, I dated pretty girls, and I had buddies. It was all fine, but something was missing. I just never knew what it was. Any gay feelings I had, I just told myself that it was normal to have feelings for other men and that it would pass. And it usually always did. It either passed or I suppressed it to the point that it was no problem. We had been married for thirteen weeks and we discovered that we were going to have a child. The marriage got off to a rocky start. I attributed it to a poor foundation and all the stresses that go along with a marriage and having a child. I'm not really sure when things began to surface with me, but probably it was not long after my wife became pregnant with our second child. I began to notice guys and have these feelings. I'd pick up the Sunday paper and see the male models and I wasn't looking at the clothes anymore. I was looking at the guys. I thought, "What's going on here? Something's just not right." Here I was sitting with my daughter on my knee, and my wife sat across the room knitting for the next child. I thought "Oh God!" It was like the worst nightmare coming true.

I really don't know how long it was between the time that I said, "Oh, I think I'm gay, and it's gonna stick" and the time I told my wife. My first encounter was with a friend of mine, Harry, that I had met before I got married. Harry was married, gay, and leading a double life. And even though I knew this, I couldn't understand how someone could let himself get in that situation. I knew him through a mutual friend, a guy that cut my hair, who had hit on me one time before I got married, and I was repulsed by it. What I've since found out is that I wasn't repulsed by the act. I was repulsed by him. He just didn't do anything for me. But at the time I didn't give it a whole lot of thought because I was getting married.

So one day I got this wild notion that I was going out of my mind with these thoughts and feelings. I felt that I had created something brand new, was the only person in the world going through this. I called Harry and asked him if we could get together and talk. Everything just came out when we talked. Harry had been in his marriage for about fourteen or fifteen years. I just couldn't understand how he could live on both sides of the fence and not tell his wife for so long. I had my first homosexual encounter with him.

Harry and I remained good friends. But about three and a half months after that, I began to feel guilty. I knew there was more to my sexuality and my being homosexual than just living the double life. After Harry, I went through a couple of brief acquaintanceships with guys—safe encounters because of AIDS. It was a year after having my experience with Harry that it all came to a head. Our marriage continued to be rocky during that time and we just attributed it to stress.

One day we were out Christmas shopping and having one of our arguments. We were having lunch in a restaurant and having an argument over something trivial. We began to talk about our relationship, what was wrong, and why it wasn't working. My wife said she knew there was something else and said that I had never opened up to her. I told her that I couldn't open up to her right then. When I said that, she picked up that there really was something else wrong that she didn't know about. She began to press me for an answer, asking, "What is it? What are you keeping from me? Why won't you tell me? Why can't we talk about it?" So in the middle of the meal I looked over at her and said, "I'm gay." She had this stunned look on her face. Tears began to roll down her face and mine, I said, "You can't begin to imagine what it's like to be a gay man, a father, respected in the community, active in the church, and be on stage all the time, and not be able to tell anyone." Her first reaction was, "Do you want a divorce?" I didn't know what I wanted. I wasn't comfortable with my feelings, so how could I expect her to be comfortable with them or to understand them?

My wife and I had been involved in an ACOA (Adult Children of Alcoholics) support group. Coming from a dysfunctional home with an alcoholic father helped me understand my sexuality but also forced me to suppress it. My wife and I went to the leader of that group for marriage counseling, and a year later we're still working on the relationship. It's not marriage like a lot of people think of a marriage. It's not a husband and wife romance. But it's not a forced relationship either. It's like we're roommates. We don't have a sexual relationship. Her interest is to keep the traditional family intact as much as possible. We're both Christian. She's even more fundamentalist than I am. There's an obligation and responsibility that says we want to stay together as a family. We want our children to grow up in as healthy an environment as possible. Sex is down on the list of priorities for both of us, even though it does crop up, and it's a problem. Sex was never a big issue with her. Her sex drive is not real strong. There are times when it is, but we don't talk about it very much. We've only been doing this for a year. I don't know how much longer the marriage will last. We've gone through therapy sessions together and separately, and she has come a long way with understanding same-sex relationships, understanding me, and understanding what it's like to be both at the same time. I've had to understand what it's like to be married to a gay man. What we're doing is taking it one day at a time. It's agreed that if it gets too much for her, I understand, and if it gets too much for me, she understands. We're both there because we want to be there. My children are extremely important to me. In the last year, I had an affair with a single gay man for a long, long time, and it was very fulfilling and satisfying. I got to the point that I couldn't do it anymore.

The incompatibility of Christianity and homosexuality was something I had to come to grips with. That was the reason that I stopped the relationship I had. There was no way in my mind as a Christian that I would ever say, "Well, I can have this relationship because I'm gay and there's nothing I can do about it." That's bull. Adultery is adultery is adultery if you consider yourself a Christian. And I knew I was committing adultery. I didn't like feeling guilty, plus I didn't like the expectations and demands he started to make on me. The guilt did not come from the homosexuality; it came from adultery. There was a long period in my life that I felt like scum just because I had these feelings.

I picked up on gay life and went through phases that normally take people five to ten years to experience. But for me it was needing to get to a comfortable level with it. I was tired of being tormented with guilt; I was tired of being tormented by my past; I was tired of living the double life. I just wanted to get somewhere that I could stop and breathe, and I think I've gotten to that point. It's a continuous thing, but at least now the person that I am today can handle whatever comes up. I'm stronger than ever. I'm not going to apologize for being gay any more than I'll apologize for having brown hair and green eyes. I have as much control over one as I do over the other. My days of sitting back and being apologetic are over. My being homosexual cannot be wrong—but what I choose to do with my homosexuality, that's what I'm responsible for. It took me a long time to get to that point, a lot of reading, soul searching, and prayer.

Nothing has ever been able to fill the place of being home with the kids and that feeling of obligation and responsibility and love that tells me that these are your children; this is where you need to be right now. When you're thirty-five they'll be almost grown. There may come a time when you can be your gay self.

When I married my wife, coming from a dysfunctional home, I was trying to create the kind of life I never had. She fit into my timetable. She was pretty, she was educated, she would be a good mother, she would make the family picture complete. But I didn't consciously realize what I was doing. I thought I was in love, but I had no basis for a healthy relationship at the time. Based on everything I had to measure from, it was love as much as I knew. At one point the concern about AIDS came up from her and me too. I've been tested for AIDS a couple of times and tested negative both times.

There was a period when I first acknowledged my sexuality that I thought that was all there was going to be in life. I just had to be in a gay relationship and experience the gay world. I went to the bars for a while and I had the relationships. Occasionally, I work on the gay/lesbian switchboard, and I have a lot of gay friends. But that's enough for me right now. Being at home with the kids, fulfilling those responsibilities, having gay friends, and being able to go to parties or have lunch with gay friends is getting enough out of it for me. What kept me in this marriage, aside from the fact that I have small children, is that I never found anything or anyone in the gay world that would make me trade what I have with my kids. And that's not to say it won't happen. My wife and I talk about our situation, occasionally we compare notes about guys we see. We even make jokes about it. We have very similar tastes in men.

We both have convictions. She was arrested this weekend in the pro-life sit in. I work the gay/lesbian switchboard. It's probably one of the healthier relationships you'll find, although it's not the "Leave it to Beaver" type family. A lot of my friends shake their heads in disbelief that I told my wife and that I'm as active with gay people as I am.

Being accepted in the gay community was a major obstacle for me to overcome. Gay married men have it worse than either straight guys or gay single guys . . . you're not accepted by heterosexuals because you're a "faggot," and you're not accepted by gay people because you're spineless and can't make a decision: "Where does your wife think you are tonight?" And that really bothered me. I always felt uneasy about that and very guilty, kind of boxed in. Where do I go? I'm gay and I'm married. I can't tell the guys down at the Y, "Hey guess what guys, I'm really struggling with being gay." And I cannot go to gay single people because most of them have absolutely no reference point for my lifestyle and where I've been. When I first came out, I was trying to approach gay life the way everybody else did. But I had to stop and realize that I will never be able to approach gay life coming from a traditional background. There's too much excess baggage that I will take into a gay relationship, being married and having kids.

When you start looking at gay married men there are many categories. You find men like myself who have told their wives. Then there are those who haven't told their wives who are extremely sexually active at the bookstores, parks, or out-of-town business trips and do not consider themselves to be gay. They set restrictions on themselves, like as long as they don't reciprocate affection they're not gay. As long as they don't kiss a man, they're not gay. There's a lot of denial, guilt, and self-justification. Two or three of my closest friends and I were common pals because we were all married and had this secret. It was always good to get together and talk. When I told my wife, I immediately felt that I was being ostracized by them: "Oh, well you've already gone way past us. You're not one of the guys anymore." That really hurt me because I didn't realize I had created a new category. I stepped one foot out of the closet and that made them very uncomfortable. They were a little resentful at first and said things like, "I guess you expect us to tell our wives now." I told them that I didn't expect them to do anything, that they would have to do what they needed to do. I wouldn't recommend this for anybody. I asked them, "Don't you care at all for your wife? Don't you have any feelings for her as a person? How can you go out and have sex at the park or bookstore and then go home and have sex with her and put her life in danger?" Obviously, things are not the same between me and my pals anymore.

The kind of relationship I have with my children now is extremely healthy and strong. I would hope that if I were thirty-five or forty years of age down the road and they were old enough to understand my sexuality that they would be accepting of it. But at the same time, realistically I know there's a risk they might not. It really hurts me that there may come a time when they may reject me even though I've sacrificed a large portion of my life to be home with them. But when you do things out of love, you do it with no expectations in return.

As far as what I teach my children about homosexuality, I don't want to differentiate heterosexual from homosexual. What I really want for my kids is for them to have an opportunity to grow up in a healthy, loving environment and whatever sexual preference they make, that's fine. But my responsibility as a parent is to provide them not with just material things, but with security, love, and happiness.

One of the greatest misconceptions is that being gay is a sexual thing. It's not by and large. Yes, there's sex to it, but that's not the whole picture. It's feelings of acceptance, closeness, and oneness with someone else. I'm not necessarily sold on the fact that homosexuality is genetic. I think your environment plays a big part in your sexuality. Based on my childhood and relationships at home, any clinical person would say, "Oh yeah, he could be gay, a pervert, a child molester. He could also be a mass murderer." My therapist said, "You know, it's really a blessing that you're just gay."

Somewhere down the road, I would like to have a special relationship with a man. If I find someone, he will have to be mentally healthy. Right now I'm exchanging the bells and whistles and skyrockets for something that's a little more comfortable. I know it's not romance, flowers, and candy, and "I love you and can't live without you." But it's also not unbearable. It's a hell of a lot better life than I had as a child. My relationship with my wife is better than it's ever been, because I'm honest for the first time. There's an understanding and a good deal of sympathy.

To clinical people who do not have a gay-positive approach or understanding, I'd like to see them more willing to listen and not make assumptions or judgments. And for God's sake, don't try to recommend a cure. There's just not one. There's no magic potion. Don't put someone through shock therapy, desensitizing them to these feelings. Gay fathers need to understand what's going on inside themselves. Maybe they need to process something in their background. Maybe they need to be told that it's okay to have these feelings. That's what they don't hear enough of. People don't say it's okay to be gay. Unfortunately, Christians are the worst. The best resource that homosexuals should be able to have, Christianity, is continually slapping them in the face. As recently as yesterday, I sat in my Sunday School class, and someone brought up a list of issues that political candidates should be concerned with. One of them was "AIDS and Homosexuals." I got up and walked out of the class. I asked my wife, "What is this about AIDS and homosexuals? Why not AIDS and heterosexuals? Or AIDS and black people? Why not just AIDS? What do they think they will do about homosexuals? Are they going to put us on another planet? I can walk back in that room right now and tell them that I'm gay. "Hi, I'm on the Board of Trustees of your church; hi, I'm Director of Children's Ministries; hi, I have a family; hi, I work for the local television station. Everybody looks at me with respect and prestige, and I'm gay. How about that, boys and girls?" There will come a time when I'll spring forth with it. But for now it's enough for me to work on it with my family. I get angry at society and at Christians who miss the greatest commandment, which is to love people. They miss the boat every time. But without having gone through being gay, I would not be as healthy as I am today. I understand why gay people in San Francisco picket and demonstrate. I understand why they're angry. They're not angry about being gay; they're angry because they live in a society that says, "Your mere existence is bad." Carry that around for about a year and a half and see how that feels. Everyday you look in the mirror, there's something wrong with you because you feel this way. Try to change it; try to make it go away. You can't imagine what it's like.

As you can already tell, every gay father's experience is different. Some men like Andrew marry and remain married, playing an important role in the child-rearing of their offspring. In many cases spouses do not know of their husband's homosexuality. In others, the wives know and tolerate their husband's lifestyle. Other wives participate in joint custody arrangements with their husbands, despite knowledge of their spouse's homosexuality. Andrew is one example of a gay father who has worked out an amicable arrangement with a wife who knows of her husband's homosexuality. Some gay fathers never marry the mother of their children. Even fewer rear their youngsters alone as single fathers because custody rulings in favor of gay men are rare, just as they are for single fathers.

Until now we have discussed the common experiences of gay fathers in order to draw a general profile. Despite these common experiences, each case has its individual characteristics and complications that require different approaches. An awareness of the varied gay father family configurations will enrich the practitioner's skills in working with gay families. In this chapter we draw a profile of gay father family types from the research literature and from our own case studies.

Demographic Information

It is impossible to give exact figures on the numbers of gay fathers in the United States. It is difficult to project the numbers of homosexual men, much less the numbers of gay fathers who live under a double risk of disclosing their sexual orientation. Still, it has been estimated that 10 percent of the adult population in the United States is gay. Statistics also suggest that 10 percent of all clients of mental health agencies are gay or lesbian (Woodman & Lenna, 1980). Of the homosexual population, projected numbers of heterosexually married gay men are approximately 20 percent (Harry, 1983). Of these marriages, approximately one-half result in children (Bell & Weinberg, 1978). Altogether, estimates are that as many as one million gay fathers live in the United States and Canada today (Bozett, 1984).

In the samples that have been studied, most of the men live separately from their spouses and see their children only periodically. Bozett (1980) reported that seventeen of the eighteen men he studied lived apart from their wives (94 percent); Miller (1979a) found that twenty-three of the forty men he interviewed lived apart from their wives (58 percent); and Skeen and Robinson (1984) reported that twenty-two of the thirty men in their study were separated or divorced from their wives (73 percent).

Gay Father Family Configurations

Being a parent is difficult enough. But research shows that being an unwed, adoptive, single, or stepparent further complicates the role. Layer any one of these roles with one or both parents being gay, and you have a set of highly complex circumstances. The stress level for gay father families is extraordinary, each family configuration with its own inherent problems. Few treatment models exist. Work with gay father families takes challenge, compassion, and creativity. Openness and flexibility are also cornerstones of the successful practitioner. The first step in intervention is for professionals to identify the family configuration of the gay father with whom they are working. Identification of family type enables workers to pinpoint unique problems, which in turn can be matched with unique solutions. Figure 3–1 shows the eight types of gay father family configu-

Figure 3–1. Gay Father Family Configurations

TYPE 1: UNMARRIED GAY FATHERS

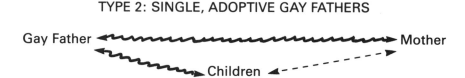

TYPE 2: SINGLE, ADOPTIVE GAY FATHERS

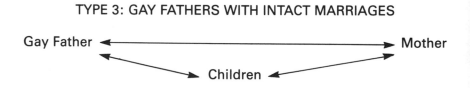

TYPE 3: GAY FATHERS WITH INTACT MARRIAGES

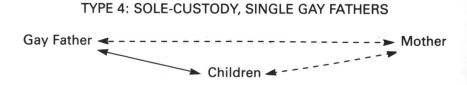

TYPE 4: SOLE-CUSTODY, SINGLE GAY FATHERS

TYPE 5: JOINT-CUSTODY, SINGLE GAY FATHERS

Gay Father — — — — — — — — — — — — — — — → Mother

Children

TYPE 6: GAY FATHER STEPFAMILIES

Gay Father ∿∿∿∿∿∿∿∿∿∿∿→ Homosexual Partner

Children

TYPE 7: SEPARATED OR DIVORCED ESTRANGED GAY FATHERS

Gay Father — — — — — — — — — — — — — — — → Mother

Children

TYPE 8: TWO GAY FATHERS AND LESBIAN MOTHER

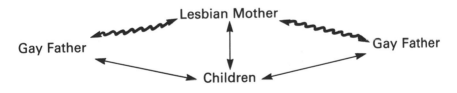

Lesbian Mother

Gay Father   Gay Father

Children

← — — — → = Intact Relationships

←∿∿∿∿→ = Nonbiological or Nonlegal Relationships

← – – – – → = Break in Relationships Caused by Separation, Death, Divorce, or Estrangement

rations. One could hypothesize that the more squiggly and broken lines in a family unit, the more inherent problems contained in that family configuration.

TYPE 1: UNMARRIED GAY FATHERS

The Type 1 family includes an unmarried gay man and woman with one or more children. This family configuration can evolve for many different reasons—each of which carries its own unique problems. The man and woman may be genuinely in love, and the pregnancy could be unplanned. The mother may or may not know of the father's sexual orientation. Practitioners involved with these cases encounter many of the same problems as those found with unplanned pregnancies and unwed parents, coupled with the factor of the father's homosexuality. Problem questions, for example, might be: "Should the couple marry, given the father's sexual orientation?" and if so, "What kinds of problems and possible solutions in such marriages can be foreseen on both sides?"

The father and mother may not be in love and neither party may desire to marry. Custody arrangements must be discussed regarding the mother's knowledge of the father's homosexuality. Some Type 1 families include preplanned pregnancies by gay men and lesbian women. These arrangements are often loosely thought out as a means for homosexual men and women to have children of their own. In some instances, the gay father and lesbian mother genuinely love one another and wish to live together, either married or unmarried. In others, the mother is artificially inseminated with the gay man's sperm. Practitioners must facilitate issues around parental responsibilities, having outside sexual partners, children's exposure to sexual partners, what to tell the children, what names to give parents' intimate partners, and how to define these intimate partners within the family. More commonly, however, practitioners deal with helping gay men and lesbian women work out a mutual, often not legally binding, custody arrangement so that both parents can share equally in the child's upbringing, since that was the original plan.

TYPE 2: SINGLE, ADOPTIVE GAY FATHERS

Malcolm is a single gay father who has never married. He adopted a ten-year-old boy and raised him as his son. In 1980, there were approximately 52,000 never-married single adopted fathers. The percentage of that number that are gay is unknown. Adoptions by heterosexual single men are very difficult because practitioners and society do not approve of single men rearing children. A man parenting a child without a wife who can provide nurturing is somehow seen as unnatural. Never-married gay men who want to adopt are especially closely scrutinized, and their sexual orientation becomes a pressing concern. Gay men who are fortunate enough to become single adoptive fathers have limited choices of school-age boys who are mentally or physically disabled, members of a minority race, delinquent, or otherwise "hard to place." Single gay foster fathers also fall into the Type 2 family category.

Practitioners are faced with helping these fathers face the usual challenge of rearing a child alone without societal support and in spite of societal disapproval. The added dimension of having a white father with a black child or the challenge of rearing a disabled or acting-out child might also have to be addressed. Professionals can combine clinical skills from two distinct areas: working with adoptive parents and parents with difficult children. Merging these skills can be modified to include special problems that relate to the father's homosexuality. Almost always this necessitates assisting the father's disclosure to an already-problemed child who is asked to accept yet another huge problem. Faced with rejection, these fathers do not have the biological ties that sometimes guarantee a parent-child bond. The "blood is thicker than water" rule does not hold in single adoptive father cases. Surprisingly though, past history in dealing with life's problems often makes it easier for these children to understand and accept their adopted father's homosexuality.

TYPE 3: GAY FATHERS WITH INTACT MARRIAGES

The Type 3 family has a gay father living with his spouse in an intact marriage with one or more children. The spouse may or may not know of her husband's homosexuality. The case of Andrew illustrates this family configuration. Although Andrew's wife knows and accepts his homosexuality, there are other situations in which wives are unaware of their husband's sexual preferences. In these instances, practitioners work predominantly with the father around issues of disclosure or nondisclosure to the spouse. With the increasing numbers of married women being infected with AIDS from bisexual or homosexual husbands, health risks and the mother's rights raise ethical issues in regard to disclosure that require resolution. Fathers need support in disclosing their sexual preferences to their spouses and in working out an equitable arrangement between them. That might include the wife's desire to continue living with her husband. In a minority of instances, practitioners find a wife who is willing to live with her husband knowing of his sexual activity. Today that arrangement is less common because of the risk of AIDS, because fewer women are willing to deny themselves a life of their own, and because fewer gay men are willing to stifle their true selves. In cases in which fathers have already told their wives, practitioners need to work with both parents around establishing an agreeable arrangement. In some situations that arrangement involves separation and divorce. When this happens, practitioners are confronted with the same issues of divorce, single parenting, and custody arrangements that occur in heterosexual marriages, layered with the complication of the father's sexual orientation.

In some Type 3 families the fathers have male partners. Practitioners find that in these circumstances, including all three adults in counseling is an added benefit to conflict resolution. Situations in which all parties can openly communicate their feelings, show empathy and compassion, and develop amicable and cooperative relationships benefit the children and help them adjust to the new family arrangement.

TYPE 4: SOLE-CUSTODY, SINGLE GAY FATHERS

The Type 4 family is one in which the gay father has sole custody of children due to separation, divorce, or death of his spouse.

This family usually occurs as a result of spousal death or the mother's willingness to give the father full custody. Custody rulings in favor of gay fathers are rare. But in 1979, a gay man did win custody of his two children, one of the first such rulings in Kansas. Upon remarrying, the children's mother (who did not want custody of her children) had become a victim of spouse abuse. The gay father said he had to take his children for therapy because of the violence they witnessed in his ex-wife's home. Before the judge ruled in the gay father's favor, two psychologists had to testify that the father's homosexuality would not cause problems of gender identity for the children.

Practitioners must handle all the issues and concerns of being a single parent in a double minority: male and gay. Single parenting brings enormous amounts of stress for men or women, but the role is further exaggerated when men must wear both hats (see, for example, Robinson & Barret, 1986). Only about 10 percent of men are custodial single fathers. The additional burden of rearing children as a homosexual father raises the level of stress to unbearable heights. Stress counseling, therefore, is a chief goal for this family type. The issue of disclosure may or may not be relevant, depending on the age of the children and the father's lifestyle. For men who insist on a gay lifestyle, a goal is to help them reconcile their lifestyle with that of rearing children in a healthy environment and dealing with societal stereotypes. The gay father in this family must face society's wrath more than in many of the other family configurations because there is no female directly involved. The Freudian belief of maternal deprivation applied against the myths of gay fathering makes this father especially vulnerable to attack.

TYPE 5: JOINT-CUSTODY, SINGLE GAY FATHERS

The Type 5 family is one in which the father is separated or divorced and shares joint custody with his wife. In some instances the gay father has not disclosed his homosexuality to his spouse, so his sexuality is not an issue in the custody decision. Although he has legal custody rights, he conceals his sexual preference and lifestyle for fear of losing parental rights. Because

custody decisions rarely allow openly gay fathers any rights,
Type 5 arrangements are usually worked out between the husband and wife, as the following example illustrates:

> Being a gay father who has chosen to share parenting on an
> equal basis with my former wife seems to many people a con-
> tradiction in lifestyles. It certainly has proved to be compli-
> cated. For me, claiming an ongoing role in the parenting pro-
> cess was a logical step. Accepting my sexual orientation and my
> desire to share life with another man meant that marriage must
> end. Both my wife and I had made a conscious decision that
> each of us wanted to be a parent. From the day she and my son
> came home from the hospital, both of us shared the joys and
> responsibilities of parenting. We consciously avoided what we
> felt to be the stereotypical parenting roles prevalent in 1973,
> the year our son was born. When our marriage ended four
> years later, it was unthinkable to me that I would give up my
> parenting role. Fortunately, my wife wanted us to continue to
> share the raising of our son. So we had no legal problems in
> establishing joint custody on an alternate week basis.

Practitioners must assist parents to make decisions regarding
custody and visitation rights. Complex issues exist on consistency
in discipline from one household to another and how to handle
arrangements when the mother has a boyfriend who may be hostile toward homosexuality. Or, if the gay father dates occasionally, the mother may have concerns over having her child exposed to intimacy between two men. The stepfather may resent
having the child spend weeks in his house after having been
"contaminated in a house full of homosexuals." Again, identical
issues that must be addressed with joint custody decisions are
confounded by issues of sexual orientation.

Type 6: Gay Father Stepfamilies

The Type 6 family is more complicated than Type 5 because the
father has a live-in male partner who essentially becomes a stepparent to the child. Many gay partners do not find such a relationship appealing to them because they must share the partner
in a complexity of relationships with children, ex-spouse, and

her new boyfriend or husband. Heterosexual stepfamilies are by nature very complex. Problems interfere with family harmony: "A host of extra people and pressures push and tug at the stepfamily, making the determination of its own destiny difficult" (Einstein, 1982, p. 7). The issue of homosexuality adds new dimensions to the problems that must be addressed. Children can become jealous and confused with their father's love interest. The father's partner must confront many of the same issues as any stepparent, plus additional hostility because he is a gay man in the position of parenting another woman's child. Often, he has entered into a family in which the gay father and his children have had a lifetime to establish their relationships. The father's partner is an outsider in many ways and may find himself having to create instant, intimate relationships with children he barely knows. They may be virtual strangers and resent each other from time to time. Mothers are often suspicious of the father's male partner and worry about the safety of their children from sexual molestation as well as the development of their children's gender identity in the company of two intimate men.

Practitioners can effectively work with this family type by using the model of stepfamily dynamics (see, for example, Robinson & Barret, 1986). Disciplining children, household rules, division of household labor, family members seeing each other undressed, sexual matters, jealousy, amount of time and attention the father distributes between his children and male partner, biological parent/stepparent/child relationships are just some of the problems that must be faced by all stepfamilies. It is important that practitioners treat the gay stepfamily as a family unit with many of the same problems as heterosexual stepfamilies, rather than as separate problems of unrelated individuals sharing a residence (Baptiste, 1987). Advising family members to seek counseling before engaging in this type of family arrangement is the best way to avoid problems. But practitioners will not always have the luxury of seeing gay stepfamilies before they have set up housekeeping. The usual custom is that families seek counseling only after problems have begun to surface. To work through problems inherent in this family type, it is crucial to include in counseling the father, his partner, the mother, her boyfriend or husband, and the children when they are at an age appropriate to benefit from inclusion. Because there are few guidelines for being a gay father with a male partner who functions as a stepparent, men in this role, along with other family members, must create their rules based on individual personalities, living arrangements, and the ages and sexes of the children. Therapists concede that agreement and unity between the biological parents is a key to minimizing conflict in stepfamilies (Visher & Visher, 1978).

TYPE 7: SEPARATED OR DIVORCED ESTRANGED GAY FATHERS

Gerard has divorced his wife and has had no contact with her or his two children in four years. This family type is one of estrangement in which spouses refuse all contact with the gay father. The children are too young to make up their own minds or they are prevented from seeing the father by the courts or the mother. Other children who are old enough to make their own decisions reject their father.

Type 7 fathers have little or no contact with their families, primarily due to their families' inability or refusal to understand and accept their sexual preference. The practitioner's clinical goals are obviously limited by this family configuration. Counseling centers around the father's feelings of rejection, alienation, isolation, and bitterness. Helping these men reach out to other fathers in similar situations can provide the needed support to ease the isolation. Sessions on self-worth and self-acceptance can also help combat their feelings of rejection.

TYPE 8: TWO GAY FATHERS AND LESBIAN MOTHER

A more atypical arrangement is one in which a lesbian woman agrees to be artificially inseminated with the mixed sperm from two gay men. This practice, usually found in larger metropolitan areas with a heavy concentration of gay men and lesbian women, results in the rearing of children who have three parents. Most of these parental threesomes do not cohabitate as a family unit, although some, like Joy Schulenburg (1985), do:

As an adult, I chose to have a child and to share that responsibility with the two gay men who are my closest friends. The four of us (Bert, Geof, daughter Veronica and I) live together as a family unit and are accepted as such by our friends and families. . . . I quickly learned to recognize my situation for what it is: a small minority within a minority group (p. 4).

Type 8 families could be a subcategory of Type 1, except for the fact that there are three parents who often live together. Although practitioners must deal with many of the same issues as in Type 1, additional unresolved questions emerge in the Type 8 family: How do three parents maintain consistency in child-rearing when it is hard enough for two to maintain uniformity? How do you explain to the kids that they have three parents instead of two? And as the child gets older, how does he or she explain that to the heterosexual world? An even further reaching question is, What happens if the three-parent family splits up and each parent goes his or her separate way? What are the custody arrangements and financial implications for such a complicated state of affairs? As you can see, there are no pat answers for these types of experimental family arrangements. But the nature of this family configuration demands creative problem solving, open dialogue among all involved parties, and frequently an objective ear to assist the family in resolving these issues.

Box 3–1
GAY PARENTS AMONG THE CASELOAD: ONE PRACTITIONER'S EXPERIENCES

I have worked with three cases involving gay parents. I had my first case when I worked in a psychiatric hospital on the adolescent unit. The daughter of a gay father came into the hospital. The fourteen-year-old, who entered the hospital for chemical dependency and conduct disorder, was in the custody of her mother. There was a lot of tension with the staff and the family because Dad was gay and living with his lover. The staff, mostly registered nurses and counselors, had a lot of difficulty adjusting to the fact that the girl's father was gay.

Negative comments were made such as, "This is unheard of, a gay father!" or "How dare he have this child in his home with his lover living there!" The staff tossed around terms like "fag" and "queer" in the hallways to refer to the girl's father. They saw Mom as the one who was trying hard and doing all the work and the father, although he paid all hospital bills, as not caring about what was going on. Under the circumstances, I felt that the father was giving as much support as he could, given the fact that he lived sixty miles away. The father's homosexuality overshadowed the real, more crucial problems in the case because it went against the staff's Southern Baptist values. Their judgmental nature interfered with the helping process for the daughter. They were unprofessional in expressing biases within earshot of other patients when their comments should have been confined to the staff areas.

They were making the fact that this child had a gay father *the* problem. But there was a lot more going on than just the fact that the girl had a gay father and there was a divorce in the family. There were a lot of interpersonal problems and peer pressure that had brought her into the substance abuse world. The biggest problems were the child's chemical dependency and feelings of depression and poor self-esteem. There were a lot of typical adolescent problems that were compounded by her drug use. The child was blatantly defiant and didn't listen to her mother.

Practitioners need to keep an open mind that there are many ways of life that they might not have grown up with. In cases such as this, staff must be more understanding of what is going on and that this is the person's chosen way to live. We must be continually aware that what's okay for this person may not be okay for us, but in that person's situation it's perfectly fine and acceptable. That's the way those clients are coping with life. If they're not having any major problems with their lifestyles, leave well enough alone. If practitioners can't handle the case, they should refer the client to someone else who they feel can better handle the case. In my own cases, I put aside whatever prejudices I have until I've read and researched the special population I'm working with. A female social worker who had the case before me couldn't wait to get rid of this case. She was happier to get rid of this case more than any other she ever gave me. It stemmed from her own discomfort, lack of knowledge, and inexperience in dealing with a gay parent.

It is important that practitioners approach gay father families in the same way as they would a heterosexual couple. When a lover is involved, that is basically a stepfamily relationship. The wrinkle in it is that Dad is living with another man and they are lovers. Being gay is not the issue. The issue is dealing with the family unit as a whole. Practitioners must alter their view to accommodate the fact that Dad is living with his lover. If it's a good relationship, don't mess with it. Leave well enough alone. What practitioners must consider is the daughter's view of what's going on and whether or not she's comfortable with it. That is an issue for individual therapy. But if Dad and his partner are comfortable and the daughter is having problems accepting their homosexuality, that's the daughter's problem and should be dealt with in individual therapy with her. If the child is having problems with Dad's male lover, that's more of a family issue, and I would treat that as I would "the wicked stepmom" problem and involve the whole family. The same goes if the "stepdad" tries to discipline the child. If it's a family problem, view it as a family problem. If it's an individual's problem, deal with it on an individual basis. But if it's not broken, don't fix it. Approach it like any other family, and if the gay issue becomes a problem, deal with it in perspective as you would any other secondary problem.

Another case was a child who had returned a second time. Her mother was a lesbian with a lover, and there were a lot of domestic problems. Although the child seemed to handle her mother's homosexuality, she didn't like the lover telling her what to do. There were several episodes when they would have knock-down, drag-out fights. The child wanted one person to discipline her. Discipline tended to be violent. The child would pull a knife or make homicidal threats to the lover. With the exception of physical violence, the underlying conflict is the same as that found in any stepfamily. We had to educate the parents about what is acceptable discipline and what is borderline child abuse. Our goal was to get the child to handle her frustrations and her feelings about the real issues of her dysfunctioning in school. We tried to get her to sit through the day without blowing up at the teacher who was telling her what to do. There was a lot of family strife, and they weren't looked upon favorably by the rest of their family. The staff also had a hard time accepting their lifestyle. It was more acceptable than the gay father family. The male staff felt more uncomfortable than the female staff.

The core issue of getting the child back into the home and dealing with the family problems was hurt by the negative comments that were made about the homosexuality. The family clashed with what the staff felt a family should be, and they were really uncomfortable with it. They viewed homosexuality as a sin and believed the clients would burn in hell for the way they were living. It was difficult for them to feel comfortable with this child's mother coming in or the mother's lover coming to pick up the child. A lot of people questioned how legal it was for the lover to sign the child out on a pass. But it was just like a "stepmom" instead of a "stepdad."

The third case was a lesbian mother who was physically abusive of her child. The child was removed from the home. Mom had a lover who also had a child that was getting most of the attention in the home. The physical abuse, though, was the key issue. Our goal was to get Mom involved with the child through family counseling and to be understanding of the daughter. Mom had a very black and white view of the world and an attitude of, "How dare you people tell me how to raise my child." She wasn't happy with the Department of Social Services (DSS) nosing in her life. She was upset with their obtrusive home visits that scrutinized her every move.

Once I acknowledged the fact that the parents were gay, there were certain issues that were different. The facts that DSS was involved and that "my lifestyle is not acceptable" had to be dealt with. At some level that had to be acknowledged and determined whether it was an issue or not. In the last case I described, it was acknowledged that the mother's lesbianism was not a problem in the family counseling sessions, but in the individual sessions with the daughter it was a problem. The daughter had a difficult time accepting the fact that her mother was in the next room sleeping with another woman. The thirteen-year-old daughter was concerned that she too might turn out to be a lesbian. The daughter was just hitting adolescence and struggling with her own sexual identity and her relationship with boys. Mom's biggest concern was that when a relationship broke up with a previous lover, her daughter would still hold an emotional attachment to her mother's former sexual partner. Mom would say, "That relationship is over and done with! Why do you keep dredging up the past?" The daughter had really bonded to one of her mother's former lovers, and this was causing some difficulty in the relationship.

The daughter wanted to go see the former lover, but Mom's view was that the lover was out of her life and therefore out of the daughter's life.

Calvin Jenner, Social Worker
Behaviorally Handicapped Group Home for Children

Tips for Practitioners

Practitioners can also be aware of the confusion and guilt that often accompany a homosexual identity within a heterosexual family setting. As we pointed out, the coming out process for gay fathers can be lengthy and painful. Putting the father's sexuality in perspective, fostering self-acceptance, providing network opportunities, and identifying gay father family types are major practitioner goals.

PUT THE FATHER'S SEXUALITY IN PERSPECTIVE

Many cases of gay fathers emerge indirectly through the primary treatment of a child or spouse. When a child or spouse is the primary client and the father has not come for treatment, practitioners must be careful not to get sidetracked by the father's sexual orientation as the central issue that directs attention away from pertinent treatment concerns. The parent's sexual orientation must be placed in perspective and addressed not as *the* problem, as is often the tendency. Instead, the gay father's sexuality can be addressed as a separate issue if, in fact, a family member is having difficulty about the homosexuality. Otherwise, treatment is fostered when practitioners focus on the relevant problems and put the parent's homosexuality in context.

WORK WITH THE FAMILY SYSTEM WHEN APPROPRIATE

Helping gay fathers may also mean helping the nuclear and extended family resolve particular issues. Family groups composed of gay fathers and their wives and children can also be useful in conflict resolution. Occasionally, professionals will be called upon to work with fathers and their male partners (and sometimes the wives) to help them work through the family transformation. Referrals to local branches of Gay Fathers Coalition is another way to achieve this end. While not the norm, some couples successfully integrate ex-spouses into their support system and often plan family meetings that include all involved parties when important decisions must be made. As spouses make decisions about custody issues and participation at family celebrations, wives, children, parents, brothers, and sisters may need to be included in counseling sessions. The family as a whole generally is involved in a crisis and may need assistance as they move through the process of integrating the newly discovered sexual orientation. One gay father reported that he was elated that his children and ex-wife would be living adjacent to him and his lover so they could all parent the children. Such mutual respect is a source of strength for children. Other parenting issues when a lover is present may include the role of the "stepfather" as well as possibly integrating families formed by two gay fathers and their children.

IDENTIFY GAY FATHER FAMILY CONFIGURATIONS

Practitioners can most effectively treat gay father families when they understand that there are many diverse types of gay father families, each type requiring different intervention approaches. Identifying the type of family configuration is important in order to match appropriate treatment goals. Once identified, a marriage and family therapy orientation similar to that used with heterosexual families works best. Drawing from work with unwed and unplanned pregnancies, adoption, single parenting, and stepfamilies, practitioners can strengthen their approach by modifying conventional marriage and family therapy techniques to include the added dimension of homosexuality. The most important point is helping professionals treat gay father families as a family unit, as they would a heterosexual family, rather than as a collection of unrelated individuals living together. Important counseling goals are helping family members clarify relationships, clarify and understand their own behaviors and interactions, and improve communication using the special nature of the relationships as leverage (Baptiste, 1987). Prior experience of working with unwed parents, adoptive and single parents, and stepparents provide many of the clinical skills practitioners need to address unique therapeutic issues of gay father families.

References

Baptiste, D. A. (1987). Psychotherapy with gay/lesbian couples and their children in "stepfamilies": A challenge for marriage and family therapists. *Journal of Homosexuality, 14,* 223–238.

Bell, A. P. & Weinberg, M. S. (1978). *Homosexualities: A Study of Diversity among Men and Women.* New York: Simon & Schuster.

Bozett, F. (1985). Gay men as fathers. In S. H. Hanson & F. W. Bozett (eds.), *Dimensions of Fatherhood.* Beverly Hills, CA: Sage, 327–352.

Bozett, F. (1984). Parenting concerns of gay fathers. *Topics in Clinical Nursing, 6,* 60–71.

Bozett, F. (1981a). Gay fathers: Evolution of the gay-father identity. *American Journal of Orthopsychiatry, 51,* 552–559.

Bozett, F. (1981b). Gay fathers: Identity conflict resolution through integrative sanctioning. *Alternate Lifestyles, 4,* 90–107.

Bozett, F. (1980). Gay fathers: How and why they disclose their homosexuality to their children. *Family Relations: Journal of Applied Family and Child Studies, 29,* 173–179.

Dank, B. M. (1971). Coming out in the gay world. *Psychiatry, 34,* 180–197.

Einstein, E. (1982). *The Stepfamily: Living, Loving, and Learning.* New York: Macmillan.

Fadiman, A. (1983). The double closet. *Life Magazine, 6,* 76–100.

Harry, J. (1983). Gay male and lesbian relationships. In E. D. Macklin, & R. H. Rubin (eds.), *Contemporary Families and Alternative Lifestyles.* Beverly Hills, CA: Sage, 216–234.

Maddox, B. (1982). Homosexual parents. *Psychology Today, 16,* 62–69.

Mager, D. (1975). Faggot father. In K. Jay & A. Young (eds.), *After You're Out.* New York: Gage.

Marciano, T. D. (1985). Homosexual marriage and parenthood should not be allowed. In H. Feldman and M. Feldman (eds.), *Current Controversies in Marriage and Family.* Beverly Hills, CA: Sage.

Miller, B. (1979a). Gay fathers and their children. *The Family Coordinator, 28,* 544–522.

Miller, B. (1979b). Unpromised paternity: Lifestyles of gay fathers. In M. Levine (ed.), *Gay Men: The Sociology of Male Homosexuality.* New York: Harper & Row.

Miller, B. (1978). Adult sexual resocialization. *Alternate Lifestyles, 1,* 207–234.

Robinson, B. E. & Barret, R. L. (1986). *The Developing Father.* New York: Guilford.

Ross, H. L. (1972). Odd couples: Homosexuals in heterosexual marriages. *Social Problems, 2,* 42–49.

Schulenburg, J. (1985). *Gay Parenting: A Complete Guide for Gay Men and Lesbians with Children.* New York: Doubleday.

Skeen, P. & Robinson, B. E. (1984). Family background of gay fathers: A descriptive study. *Psychological Reports, 54,* 999–1005.

Visher, E. B. & Visher, J. S. (1978). Common problems of stepparents and their spouses. *American Journal of Orthopsychiatry, 48,* 252–262.

Woodman, H. J. & Lenna, H. R. (1980). *Counseling with Gay Men and Women: A Guide for Facilitating Positive Life Styles.* San Francisco: Jossey-Bass.

Wyers, N. L. (1987). Homosexuality in the family: Lesbian and gay spouses. *Social Work, 32,* 143–148.

4

Children of Gay Fathers

THE CASE OF CALLIE, THE DAUGHTER OF A GAY FATHER

Callie, thirteen, and her brother Chip, seventeen, live in a joint custody situation with their parents, who are divorced. Their mother is accepting and supportive of their father's sexual orientation.

When I was in sixth grade my dad explained to me about being gay, and it never really bothered me. I really don't know how it would be different living with a straight father because this is all I've ever had. I don't know what my friends' fathers are like, but I know they're real nice too. It's hard for me to hear people talking about gay people at school, when they don't even know anything about them to say anything. I really don't pay too much attention to them. I just think, "If they only knew. . . ." I sort of feel that I'm lucky to have this opportunity that they'll never have or understand—what being gay really is. It's given me the chance to find out what it's really like. If I were somebody who was brought up in a prejudiced family, saying things that aren't true about gay people, I wouldn't ever find out what it's really like. I feel it's special for me to be in this situation with a gay father.

I've never had anybody to tell to be embarrassed about my dad. My friends don't know. They think he's a single father. When my dad had lovers, I always told my friends that he's renting a room out and he's a real good friend of ours. And they understand that completely. If I could change my father and make him straight, I wouldn't do it because I like him just the way he is.

The bad thing about it is that I can't tell anybody because I don't know if they would understand. I would like to be able to tell a close friend things that happen, but I can't really risk that. I have some very good friends, but I don't know how they feel about gays. Most of my friends are not prejudiced and they don't really care, but you just can't go out and start talking about it. The good thing is that things are so open in my family. You don't have to hide anything from each other. Some fathers don't even tell their family they are gay. We have such a good relationship. I think knowing Dad is gay brings us closer together. Some fathers are closed and are not very open with their family.

I don't know what I'd do without him. He's always there when you need him and he's so understanding, just like a best friend. You can talk to him anytime you need to. It's great! I don't know what it would be like being with another kind of father. I talk about my dad all the time, but my friends never talk about theirs. When they do talk about them, I get the feeling that they're not as close to them. They talk about their dads watching the game on TV.

I've had trouble listening to people talking about gay people. I had an orchestra teacher once who talked about it. Before he would conduct, he'd make it clear that he was married and had kids so we wouldn't get any ideas that he was gay—because he had kids. That really bugged me because he started bad mouthing gay people, and it hurt. It was like he was putting down my dad, even though he wasn't saying it directly to me. It was just like a big put down. I have trouble with that. The teacher doesn't know anything. To think that people grow up not learning anything when they think they do—not just about gays but about other religions, blacks, or anyone different, and they start talking about them, and they don't even know what they're talking about. And that bugs me!

Gay people are no different from anybody else. They don't act any different or look any different and in a lot of ways they're friendlier. Not because they're gay but because they're more open and comfortable around us. When Dad has a lover I don't feel threatened. I probably would if my dad had another woman or my mom another man. Maybe because I would think that they would try to play a role. Another woman might try to become my mother. That's sort of how I think it would be. I don't know why, but it just seems that way to me. But when Dad holds hands with another man or puts his arm around him, it doesn't bother me. It looks normal to me.

When I walk into Dad's house, this is life for me, and when I walk out, I know what I'm supposed to be handling out there. I deal with the gay world in here—with my dad and his friends—and then when I'm with my friends, I deal with it their way. It's kind of like I'm split in half almost. It doesn't bother me unless my friends or people say bad things about it. I think it's a bunch of nonsense that just because my dad is gay it will make me gay. I think people are either born gay or they're not. I don't think that if your dad is gay, you're going to be gay. You can't choose if you're going to be gay. You can't make somebody be gay. You just are what you are. And I guess people just grow up thinking that if your dad is gay, you're going to be gay too. I'm attracted to boys; I'm not gay.

People who don't understand should get to know some gay people. They'll see that gay people are not so terrible. Don't judge them for what sex they choose to be with, or their hair, or their appearance. Judge them for their personality, for who they are. When two men are in love, there's nothing wrong with it. They're just in love, and that's okay. Most people think that being gay is only the sexual part of it. They don't think they're in love. They think they're dirty and they're child molesters and things like that. But, like, what are the percentages? People should just know that it's a love relationship also. I get very angry at people who don't understand. Sometimes I feel like screaming at them, "Shut up! You don't know what you're talking about!" There are people out there with feelings. There could be a gay student in this class. You shouldn't be saying anything at all about gay people. It could be just tearing them apart because you said that.

Often the children of gay fathers are seen as innocent victims. But such an attitude is simply one more case of homophobia. The children of gay fathers are like all children—those who have fathers who love them and create close relationships with them seem to get along just fine. Those with fathers who are distant, rejecting, or suffer from other psychological problems are likely to develop problems as well. As Callie talked with us, she covered most of the issues relevant to the children of gay fathers. Some of the myths discussed in earlier chapters run rampant here. Concerns are typically expressed about the likelihood that children raised in gay families will become homosexuals themselves or that the gay parent will attempt to seduce the same-sex child. As we already have stated, research indicates that both of these myths are simply not supported in actual life. Children in gay families are as well-adjusted as all kids. They excel in school, sports, and other extracurricular activities, and they have drug and alcohol problems, get pregnant, don't apply themselves to schoolwork—just like all young people. In short, there is no indication that having a gay father is necessarily an impairment.

Concerns continue to negatively impact the relationships that gay fathers can create with their children. Before examining the parenting styles of gay fathers, this chapter will provide a brief review of the research findings relative to homosexual incest and the fear of "catching" homosexuality.

Homosexual Incest

The notion that gay men as fathers will sexually molest their children is one of the most frequently cited rationales for denying custody. Before exploring the limited literature on the topic, it is important to remember that research on gay fathers is severely limited by the few studies and the complex methodological issues involved in such efforts. These are addressed more directly in chapter 7.

In recent years, research on incest has brought renewed attention to this topic. Yet, studies on incest involving homosexuals continue to be scant; this may be a reflection of the few gay men who participate in incest or a reflection of the strong taboo against talking about such sexual contacts. As we stated earlier, child molesters and incest perpetrators are generally heterosexual men. Gay parents and their lovers are involved in virtually no cases of child sexual abuse (Geiser, 1979; DeFrancis, 1976; Gebhard, Gagnon, Pomeroy & Christenson, 1965; Richardson, 1981). Whereas definitive conclusions cannot be drawn at this time, it appears that children living with gay parents are at less risk of sexual abuse than children with heterosexual parents.

Some people fear that children living in gay households will "catch" homosexuality from their parent (the germ theory of homosexuality). Others worry that these children have a congenital predisposition toward homosexuality that is effectively curbed by placing them in heterosexual environments (Miller, 1979). Based in part on psychoanalytic and social learning theories that emphasize the major role of the same-sex and opposite-sex parent in psychosexual development, proponents of this position ignore both the heterosexuality of children raised in single-parent households and the homosexuality of children raised by heterosexual parents. Research does not support either of the concerns (Green, 1978; Miller, 1979). While most of the studies on "catching" homosexuality involve lesbians as subjects, the consensus does not support the contention that homosexuality is transmitted from lesbian mothers or from gay fathers to their children (Pennington, 1987; Steckel, 1987).

The concerns that gay fathers will either molest their children or pass along their homosexuality to them reflect an underlying negative attitude about homosexuality—that homosexuals are somehow more sexually undependable with their children than heterosexuals and that homosexuality would be a "bad" thing to catch. Many gay fathers point to the heterosexuality of their own families of origin as a refutation of this concern. One gay father said, "Claiming my sons would catch homosexuality from me is an outrage. If that's the way people become gay, I would be straight. Using this as an excuse to keep my kids from me is just another example of homophobia!" The scant research on these topics indicates that gay fathers do not attempt to influence their children to become homosexuals and that the sexual preference of the father has little bearing on the child's sexuality (Weeks, Derdeyn & Langman, 1975).

Influences on Children

In reviewing the impact of gay fathering on children, it is important to acknowledge that most children who live with gay fathers are also the products of divorce and may present psychological distress that typically accompanies families experiencing marital dissolution. All too often the emotional distress of children with gay parents is solely attributed to the parents' sexual orientation rather than seen as a complex mixture of family dynamics, divorce adjustment, and incorporation of the parents' sexual coming out.

There are, of course, many issues that are unique to living in a family with a gay father. There are legitimate concerns about the developmental impact of the knowledge that one's father is homosexual, reasonable questions about the need for coming out to one's children, and essential awarenesses to develop about ways to assist children to minimize the difficulties created by society's negative attitudes about homosexuality. Callie's story at the beginning of the chapter touches on these three issues. There is a possible element of defensiveness in her story that indicates that her overt statements accepting and even prizing her father's sexual orientation may mask a deeper anxiety over how she will cope with this issue as she participates in normal adolescent activities related to her own unfolding sexual relationships with males. Let's examine each of these issues to see how they are experienced.

Coming Out to Children

Coming out to their children is typically an emotion-laden event for gay fathers. Disclosing one's homosexuality to children generates anxiety about possible rejection, fear of damaging the child's self-esteem, and often an awareness that the relationship is about to undergo a fundamental change and a kind of fathering will have been lost forever. One father told us:

> I knew that my children had not asked to have a father who is gay, and I just could not bring myself to tell them until they became adults. I hoped that by then they would be successfully launched into life and that my lifestyle would have little impact on them. After I first told them they were really angry with me. Finally two of them have come around and seem to want to be a part of my life. The other two are still somewhat wary and reserved. If I could be twenty again, I would probably still

marry and have children, for my life with my wife and kids has been deeply meaningful to me. I would not trade the twenty-eight years I spent with them for anything. But, now they have their own lives, and I can finally live more of my own life too.

A sixty-one-year-old gay father said:

My married daughter walked in on me when I was kissing my twenty-six-year-old boyfriend one night. Neither of us said anything about it; she just walked out of the room. I suppose that she has told my son about it. I'll never talk with them about it, and after that happened, I decided I'll never live with a male lover again. Somehow I hope to keep up the front of being heterosexual.

The daughter of another gay father said:

I did not want my father to talk with me about being gay. I knew he was, and I felt violated by that conversation. It would have been easier for me if we had never talked about it. He keeps insisting that I tell him how I feel about it. I just don't want to discuss it at all. I resent it when he brings it up, and sometimes I don't want to be around him.

No one knows how many gay fathers actually do come out to their children. Although they may have come out to themselves and to other members of the gay community and may be involved in clandestine affairs with men, many cite legal and emotional reasons for staying in the closet (Bozett, 1980, 1981; Humphreys, 1970; Spada, 1979). Others feel their family roles cannot be reconciled with their sexual orientation and never disclose (Bozett, 1981; Jones, 1978; Ross, 1971). These men lead deeply conflicted lives and probably project their internalized homophobia onto their children as they state, "I am staying married just for my children." Their parenting is characterized by psychological distance, they tend to be more indulgent as a means of resolving some of the guilt they feel over their lack of honesty, and many become workaholics (Miller, 1979).

Those fathers who do disclose their sexual orientation do so for a variety of reasons. One man told us, "I like myself as a gay

Box 4-1
COMING OUT TO CHILDREN: GUIDELINES FOR FATHERS

Bigner and Bozett (1990) draw from the work of Miller (1979) and Schulenburg (1985) in their presentation of some Principles for Disclosure of Homosexuality to Children. These very practical suggestions will be helpful to gay fathers, their children, and mental health professionals.

1. *Come to terms with your own gayness before disclosing to children.* This is crucial. The father who feels negatively about his homosexuality or is ashamed of it is much more likely to have children who also react negatively. The father must create a setting of acceptance by first accepting himself. If he tells his children when he is ready and comfortable, it is likely to be a positive experience for everyone.

2. *Children are never too young to be told.* They will absorb only as much as they are capable of understanding. Use words appropriate to the age of the child. Details may be added as they grow older.

3. *Discuss it with children before they know or suspect.* When children discover their father's sexual orientation from someone other than the father, they often are upset that their father did not trust them sufficiently to share the information with them. It is exceedingly difficult for children to initiate the subject, and they will not bring it up even though they want to.

4. *Disclosure should be planned.* Children should not find out about their father's homosexuality by default or discover it accidentally or during an argument between their parents.

5. *Disclose in a quiet setting where interruptions are unlikely to occur.*

6. *Inform, don't confess.* The disclosure should not be heavy or maudlin but positive and sincere. Informing in a simple, natural, and matter-of-fact manner when the father is ready is more likely to foster acceptance by the child. If

Bigner, J. J. & Bozett, F.W. (1990). Parenting by gay fathers. *Marriage and Family Review*, in press.

possible, discuss or rehearse what will be said to children with someone who has already experienced a similar disclosure.

7. *Inform the children that relationships with them will not change as a result of disclosure.* Disclosure will, however, allow the father to be more honest. Children may need reassurance that the father is the same person he was before. Younger children may need reassurance that the father will still be their father.

8. *Be prepared for questions.* Some questions and possible answers are:

   - *Why are you telling me this?* Because my personal life is important and I want to share it with you. I am not ashamed of being homosexual, and you shouldn't be ashamed of me either.

   - *What does being gay mean?* It means being attracted to other men so that you might fall in love with a man and express your love physically and sexually.

   - *What makes a person gay?* No one knows, although there are a lot of theories. (This question may be a child's way of asking if he or she will also be gay.)

   - *Will I be gay, too?* You won't be gay just because I'm gay. It's not contagious, and it doesn't appear to be hereditary. You will be whatever you are going to be.

   - *Don't you like women?* (The child might be asking, "Don't you like Mom?" or "Do you hate Mom?" If this question is asked by a daughter it may also mean, "Don't you like me?" or "Do you hate me?") I do like women but I'm not physically (or sexually) and romantically attracted to them as I am to men.

   - *What should I tell my friends about it?* A lot of people just don't understand so it might be best to keep it in the family. You can discuss it with me any time you want. If you want to tell a close friend, go ahead and try it out. But the friend might not be accepting, and she or he might tell others. You should be prepared for those possibilities. If you do tell somebody, let me know how it turns out.

man. It is only natural to want to share that part of who I am with my kids. They will learn something quite valuable from knowing this part of me." This father's comment is consistent with findings that indicate gay fathers value their role as father (Bozett, 1980) and also their sexual identity. As they come to also value themselves as homosexuals, it is natural that they would want to share this aspect of themselves with their children. Once a gay man begins to overcome his own internalized fear and shame about being homosexual, he becomes more integrated, and he often reveals his sexual orientation to others. Coming out is one part of developing a positive gay identity, and coming out to one's children is seen as an essential part of having integrity as a parent.

As these fathers face coming out, their first concern is the well-being and healthy adjustment of their children. Their second worry is that their children, perhaps their major intimate relationship, will reject them. Study after study indicates that, in fact, children and fathers report they are closer after self-disclosure about the father's sexual orientation (Bozett, 1980; Miller, 1979). Several years after learning his father is a homosexual, Jim said:

> I never knew much about gay men. From my Dad I've learned that gay people are just like all people. I like some of them and don't like others. My likes and dislikes have little to do with their gayness and more to do with who they are. I can see that Dad is happier and that's what is most important. He has introduced me to people and activities I would have never known about otherwise, and I've learned not to be so judgmental about people who are different.

Coming out is influenced by several factors. Bigner and Bozett (1990) report that the men they studied weigh several factors as they decide to come out. Wanting their children to know them as they are, being aware that the more frequent the contact the greater the likelihood children will discover on their own, and the presence of a male lover are given as major reasons for disclosure. Children may also benefit from this information as they are able to understand what went wrong in the marriage and often no longer feel responsible for the divorce (Miller, 1979).

Gay fathers may come out indirectly (showing affection to men in front of their children or taking their children to gay restaurants and meetings) or directly (verbally or by correspondence), the process that is most preferred (Maddox, 1982). Some disclosure may take place over time as the father develops a more positive gay identity (Bozett, 1984) and as the family begins to adjust to the divorce (Bozett, 1981; Collins & Zimmerman, 1983; Gochros, 1985). Other factors in disclosure are the degree of intimacy between the father and his children and the obtrusiveness of his gayness (Bozett, 1988). Children who are told at an earlier age are reported to have fewer difficulties managing the knowledge of their father's homosexuality (Bozett, 1989).

Randy, a gay father, has not yet told his eight-year-old daughter that he is gay even though his ex-wife knows about it, and he lives with his lover, Bill.

> I had worried about being attracted to men, but girls chased me throughout high school and college. Sex with them was okay, and I didn't have anyone to talk with. I got married when I was twenty, and Bethany was born two years later. On a business trip I found myself having sex with a man, and I knew for sure that I was gay. I didn't tell Mary [my wife] for a while. Instead, I went to my minister and talked with him about it. He had me read the Bible and pray for the feelings to go away. I tried so hard, but could not stay away from men. Mary and I drifted further apart and I was not surprised when she told me she had fallen in love with someone else and wanted a divorce. That seemed like the perfect solution for both of us. Later, I found out that after I talked with him [the minister] he called Mary in and told her about me, but we've never talked about it. I have Bethany with me one weekend a month and I see her each week even though they live seventy miles from here. I am grateful Mary has not stood in the way of my being with my daughter. I can't imagine how I will ever tell Bethany about me. Recently my lover has been talking about trying to become heterosexual, and our relationship is changing. He is patient when Bethany is here, but he doesn't really like having her around. I worry about what is ahead for all of us.

As Bethany gets older her awareness of her father's lifestyle is certain to grow. How the two of them will negotiate his disclosure is uncertain. But it is equally unfortunate that when he turned to a professional for help, his trust was betrayed. It is doubtful that he will be willing to seek assistance when the day for coming out arrives.

Parenting Styles

Findings from the research suggests that parenthood is experienced for similar reasons for both gay and heterosexual men (Bigner & Jacobsen, 1989a). But gay fathers try harder to create stable home lives and positive relationships with their children than one would expect from traditional heterosexual parents (Bozett, 1989). Children living in families with a homosexual parent present themselves with the same issues that one would observe in children living in more conventional families. Harris and Turner (1986) interviewed twenty-three gay and lesbian parents and sixteen heterosexual single parents and found few differences in their parenting. Both homosexual and heterosexual subjects reported only minimal serious problems and characterized their relationships with their children as mostly positive. The only noticeable difference was an increased concern among heterosexual parents for their children's exposure to an opposite-sex role model. These researchers conclude that being homosexual is compatible with effective parenting and is not usually a major issue in parental relationships with children.

Another study comparing gay and heterosexual fathers found that gay men were more nurturing, less traditional in paternal attitudes, and describe themselves as functioning more positively as fathers than heterosexual fathers (Scallen, 1981). Although heterosexual fathers in this study placed more emphasis on their role as economic provider, no differences between the two groups were reported on parental problem solving, recreation, or encouragement of autonomy.

In another study of gay fathers, Bigner and Jacobsen (1989b) found no differences on parental involvement and amount of intimacy in the sixty-six fathers they sampled (thirty-three homosexual, thirty-three heterosexual). Gay fathers in this study differed significantly in that they used more reasoning, were more responsive to their children's behaviors, and were more strict in setting limits for their children. The investigators attributed their findings to possible beliefs among gay fathers that they must be better parents to overcome potential hardships resulting from the father's sexuality. They must run a tight ship in the execution of their control over their kids because they feel they are being examined more closely than other fathers because of their sexual orientation. These conclusions are similar to the experience of noncustodial single fathers reported elsewhere (Robinson & Barret, 1986).

Findings of no difference between homosexual and heterosexual fathers do not mean that the experience of having a gay father is risk free. Miller (1979) found that six daughters of the gay fathers in his study had significant life problems (pregnancy, prostitution, school, and emotional difficulties). Other reports indicate that children with gay fathers are exposed to ridicule and harassment (Bozett, 1980; Epstein, 1979) or may become alienated from their agemates, become confused about their sexual identity, and express discomfort with their fathers' sexual orientation (Lewis, 1980). Remember that these responses may not be solely related to the sexuality of the father; these children have lost whatever stability their family life offered them. Their problems are surely a result of adjusting to a mixture of very complex issues at crucial developmental phases.

Dealing With the Outside World

Gay fathers and their children live in a larger world, one that is definitely not hospitable to gay men and lesbians and certainly not generally supportive of gay parenting. One facet of coming out as a gay father is planning ways to successfully interact with the world of schools, PTAs, churches, scouts, athletic and cultural events, and social networks. Adapting to the realities of a homophobic world, gay fathers often see no choice other than to continue living relatively closeted lives (Miller, 1979; Bozett, 1988). Helping their children develop a positive attitude about homosexuality conflicts with the caution against letting teachers and friends know about their fathers' homosexuality. Some deal with this by placing their children in schools outside the neighborhood (Strommen, 1989). Others, fearing the exposure of a possible custody battle based on their homosexuality, live tightly controlled lives or simply never develop their gay identity. The overall thrust, however, is one to protect their children from the adverse effects that often follow public disclosure. At the same time, many of these fathers attempt to help their children develop a positive gay sensitivity as opposed to taking on society's negative homosexual labeling (Morin & Schultz, 1978; Riddle, 1978).

Bozett (1988) identified several strategies that children employ as they encounter their own and the public's discomfort with gay fathers. Based on the theoretical underpinnings of attribution (Kelley, 1967) and stigma (Goffman, 1963), Bozett found that children of gay fathers utilize boundary control (control of the father in relation to the self, control of the self in relation to the father, and control of others in relation to the father), nondisclosure, and disclosure strategies as they interact with their gay fathers and the outside world. Major reasons subjects gave for not disclosing their fathers' gayness included the fear that their identity would become contaminated by their peers thinking that if their father is gay, they must be gay, too. Interviews with children of gay parents indicate that children who do disclose often are taunted by being called "queer" and "fag." This concern is particularly evident when the children are in their adolescent years (Riddle & Arguelles, 1981). The social control strategy selected is influenced by the degree of intimacy between parent and child, whether the child resides with the father or not, and the maturity of the child.

Obviously, children with gay fathers must carefully consider the consequences as they decide who and how to inform others of their fathers' sexual orientation. Keeping this important aspect of their lives secret means they will live highly compartmentalized lives and that they may present feelings of isolation and alienation as they seek mental health services.

Conclusions

In summary, the limited research findings indicate that children of homosexual fathers do not differ significantly from children reared in more traditional families. They appear to accept their fathers as gay and find ways to integrate this uniqueness into their lives. The following conclusions can be drawn about children of homosexual fathers:

- They are like all kids. Some will excel, some will have problems, some will be average.
- They face a significantly different home environment and must develop strategies to deal with it.
- They may need help sorting out their own feelings about homosexuality.
- They may be isolated and angry.
- They are not likely to become homosexual.
- They are in little danger of sexual abuse.
- Many of them adjust to this family system and use it to learn about an aspect of humanity they might otherwise ignore.
- There is an opportunity for them to become not only tolerant of but also supporters of a positive gay identity.
- Their relationships with their fathers are reported as being more honest and open.

Tips for Practitioners

Mental health professionals who interact with children of gay fathers need to be prepared much in the same way fathers prepare themselves for disclosure. (Refer to Box 4–1.) It is important to reflect the potential for developing positive attitudes toward homosexuality as an alternative lifestyle that has a unique richness and diversity about it. Such gay positiveness combined with a realistic expression of the difficulties inherent in any alternative lifestyle will enable the child to explore all aspects of his or her situation. The following guidelines represent a synthesis of this chapter.

HELP CHILDREN SEPARATE SEXUAL ISSUES FROM DIVORCE ISSUES

The child's emotional crisis is likely to be based in a complex reaction to a major life change. Feelings related to the parental separation or divorce as well as to the father's sexuality are likely to be intertwined. Carefully help the child separate these issues by exploring the extent to which each situation is distressing. Further, the reactions of parents and the extended families can serve as secure anchors or sources of distress for children. For example, children caught in the crossfire of one family system that wants to totally exclude their father and another that either tolerates or welcomes him may report conflicted loyalties. Their distress may be more related to this disparity than to their father's sexuality. In any major change children will benefit from the maintenance of routines that allow them to experience predictability and control. Access to both parents during this change will be stabilizing.

INFORM CHILDREN ABOUT THE GRIEVING PROCESS

Children, like adults, may need help sorting out their own feelings about homosexuality (based on their own experiences) and the negative stereotype so prevalent throughout the world. Providing information about homosexuality and gay fathers appropriate to the age of the child will be helpful. Adjustment to any life change is a process. It is important to validate and legitimize whatever feelings children may present as their reaction to what has happened. At the same time it could help to let them know that this adjustment is part of an ongoing process and that they may develop quite different feelings over time. Expressions of anger and betrayal at the father for his deception need exploration. Issues of grief and loss over the nuclear family as well as the father's heterosexuality may also be anticipated.

HELP RESOLVE CONFLICT BETWEEN INNER FEELINGS AND SOCIETY'S STANDARDS

Assistance will be needed in resolving the disparity between society's negative message about homosexuals and filial love. Many of these children are in a bind as they express feelings of love for their fathers while at the same time they recognize that the world at large does not respect them. Helping children realize that being homosexual is more than simply having sex with men is the first step in introducing them to the diversity inherent in this subculture. Presenting the gay family as one part of the spectrum of the alternative lifestyles movement of the late 1900s will put the child's experience in perspective. For example, encouraging the child to identify the different types of families he or she has been exposed to will be reassuring.

ALLAY CHILDREN'S FEARS OF HOMOSEXUALITY AND HOMOPHOBIA

Children may need to be reassured that their fathers' sexual orientation does not automatically mean that they will be homosexual also. Children may need help formulating responses to inquisitive outsiders as well as support in keeping their fathers' homosexuality a secret. Children also may need help in exploring ways to communicate their feelings in a direct manner. Learning how to sensitize their fathers to their discomfort at observing men kissing or other physical expressions of affection between men or learning how to stand up for themselves in the new family system may be necessary.

FACILITATE THE COMING-OUT PROCESS

Prior to involvement with children, mental health professionals may find themselves assisting a gay father to plan his coming out to his children. Having him examine how to give this information as well as expressing what he needs from them are two important parts of this process. It will be helpful to encourage him to rehearse what he will say in the counselor's presence.

USE ROLE MODELS

Some children live with gay parents who chose parenting in full awareness of their homosexuality. These children grow up in households where the father's homosexuality has been a daily part of their lives. Openly gay men who become parents through surrogate mothers, adoption, or other legal means typically are focused on the well-being of their children but also are less afraid of losing custody if their sexual orientation becomes known. These families often can serve as role models for other gay families.

PROVIDE SUPPORT GROUPS FOR CHILDREN

Many of these children live in families that have become isolated from the mainstream. Their reactions to being different often cause them to not include their peers in their home environments. Referring them to a support group for children in gay families can reduce some of their isolation. If such groups are not available, giving them information about the existence of these groups in other cities can help "normalize" their experience. Some gay fathers also become isolated because they fear disclosure would mean a loss of custody. These families may devote significant energy to "keeping the secret." That can include sending children to schools out of the neighborhood or having no social life that incorporates their home lives. Use the resources in the Appendix to help children contact organizations or literature that will give them more perspective on their situations.

FOCUS ON SIMILARITIES RATHER THAN DIFFERENCES

Recognizing that gay families are very similar to more traditional families is important. Gay families show evidence of love and concern just like other families; they adjust to divorce just like other families; and their postdivorce reorganization creates similar strains and opportunities. The gay family can be a source of growth for all who encounter it and can serve as a most appropriate learning forum for developing respect for all types of people.

References

Bigner, J. & Bozett, F. W. (1990). Parenting by gay fathers. *Marriage and Family Review,* in press.
Bigner, J. & Jacobsen, R. B. (1989a). The value of children to gay and heterosexual fathers. *Journal of Homosexuality, 18,* 163–172.

Bigner, J. & Jacobsen, R. B. (1989b). Parenting behaviors of homosexual and heterosexual fathers. *Journal of Homosexuality, 18,* 173–186.

Bozett, F. W. (1989). Gay fathers: A review of the literature. *Journal of Homosexuality, 18,* 137–162.

Bozett, F. W. (1988). Social control of identity by children of gay fathers. *Western Journal of Nursing Research, 10,* 550–565.

Bozett, F. W. (October, 1984). "The Children of Gay Fathers: Strategies for Coping with Identity Variance." Paper presented at the National Council on Family Relations, San Francisco, CA.

Bozett, F. W. (1981). Gay fathers: Evolution of the gay father identity. *American Journal of Orthopsychiatry, 51,* 552–559.

Bozett, F. W. (1980). Gay fathers: How and why they disclose their homosexuality to their children. *Family Relations, 29,* 173–179.

Collins, L. & Zimmerman, N. (1983). Homosexual and bisexual issues. In J. C. Hansen, J. D. Woody & R. H. Woody (eds.), *Sexual Issues in Family Therapy.* Rockville, MD: Aspen Publications, 82–100.

DeFrancis, V. (1976). *Protecting the Child Victim of Sex Crimes Committed by Adults.* Denver: American Humane Society, Children's Division.

Epstein, R. (June, 1979). Children of gays. *Christopher Street,* 43–50.

Gebhard, P., Gagnon, J., Pomeroy, W. & Christenson, C. (1965). *Sex Offenders: An Analysis of Types.* New York: Harper & Row.

Geiser, R. L. (1979). *Hidden Victims: The Sexual Abuse of Children.* Boston: Beacon Press.

Gochros, J. S. (1985). Wives' reactions to learning that their husbands are bisexual. *Journal of Homosexuality, 11,* 101–113.

Goffman, E. (1963). *Stigma.* Englewood Cliffs, NJ: Prentice-Hall.

Green, R. (1978). Sexual identity of 37 children raised by homosexual or transsexual parents. *American Journal of Psychiatry, 135,* 692–697.

Harris, M. B. & Turner, P. H. (1986). Gay and lesbian parents. *Journal of Homosexuality, 12,* 101–113.

Humphreys, L. (1970). *Tearoom trade.* Chicago: Aldine.

Jones, C. (1978). *Understanding Gay Relatives and Friends.* New York: Seabury Press.

Kelley, H. (1967). Attribution theory in social psychology. In D. Levine (ed.), *Nebraska Symposium on Motivation (Vol. 15).* Lincoln: University of Nebraska.

Lewis, K. (1980). Children of lesbians. Their point of view. *Social Work, 25,* 200.

Maddox, B. (1982, February). Homosexual parents. *Psychology Today,* 62–69.

Miller, B. (1979, October). Gay fathers and their children. *The Family Coordinator, 28,* 544–551.

Morin, S. & Schultz, S. (1978). The gay movement and the rights of children. *Journal of Social Issues, 34,* 137–148.

Pennington, S. B. (1987). Children of lesbian mothers. In F. W. Bozett (ed.), *Gay and Lesbian Parents.* New York: Praeger.

Richardson, D. (1981). Lesbian mothers. In J. Hart & D. Richardson (eds.), *The Theory and Practice of Homosexuality.* London: Routledge & Kegan Paul.

Riddle, D. (1978). Relating to children: Gays as role models. *Journal of Social Issues, 34,* 38–58.

Riddle, D. & Arguelles, M. (1981). Children of gay parents: Homophobia's victims. In I. Stuart & L. Abt (eds.), *Children of Separation and Divorce.* New York: Van Nostrand Reinhold.

Robinson, B. E. & Barret, R. L. (1986). *The Developing Father: Emergent Roles in Contemporary Society.* New York: Guilford.

Ross, L. (1971). Mode of adjustment of married homosexuals. *Social Problems, 18,* 385–393.

Scallen, R. (1981). "An Investigation of Paternal Attitudes and Behaviors in Homosexual and Heterosexual Fathers." Doctoral dissertation, California School of Professional Psychology. *Dissertation Abstracts International, 42,* 3809B.

Schulenburg, J. (1985). *Gay Parenting.* Garden City, NY: Doubleday.

Simari, C. G. & Baskin, D. (1982). Incestuous experiences within homosexual populations: A preliminary study. *Archives of Sexual Behavior, 11,* 329–344.

Spada, J. (1979). *The Spada Report,* New York: Signet Books.

Steckel, A. (1987). Psychosocial development of children of lesbian mothers. In F. W. Bozett (ed.), *Gay and Lesbian Parents.* New York: Praeger.

Strommen, E. (1989). "You're a what?": Family member reactions to the disclosure of homosexuality. *Journal of Homosexuality, 18,* 37–58.

Voeller, B. & Walters, J. (1978). Gay fathers. *The Family Coordinator, 27,* 149–157.

Weeks, R., Derdeyn, A. & Langman, M. (1975). Two cases of children of homosexuals. *Child Psychiatry and Human Development, 6,* 26–32.

5

Parents and Wives of Gay Fathers

The Case of Ruth the Mother of a Gay Father

As my son grew up, I often wondered if he might be gay. He was not very sports-minded, and as a child he liked to play with his cousin, Sharon, more than with other boys. He was a good student and in high school he dated a lot, so I quit worrying about it after a while. He was different from his brothers, we all knew that. He was married for over twenty years, and I could tell that he was a good father to his two sons. Even when they were babies, he liked taking care of them, and he always talked about them. I sensed that things were not always right between him and his wife, but I stayed out of it. Living 700 miles away, I only saw them a couple of times a year, but I knew something was wrong. Jim was just not happy, and I couldn't figure out why. He changed jobs a lot and didn't have friends like his brothers. He liked fixing up old houses and going to art galleries—things that most men in our family never were interested in. When he left a good paying job to become a teacher, I thought he had lost his mind. He would never make any money in the school system. Of course, he didn't listen to us. I could see that he liked working with the kids at his school, but still something was just not right. The boys grew up and went off to college, and suddenly things just fell apart.

When he called to tell me that he was leaving his wife, I was not really surprised. They were so different, and I had worried that once the boys were gone they would have some hard times. She had her work and would be okay, but I couldn't imagine how he would get along by himself. Once I asked him if there were reasons I did not know about that caused his marriage to fail. When he said yes, I told him I didn't want to know what they were. But in my heart I knew that he was gay, and I dreaded the day when he would tell me about that. I had never known any gay people and couldn't imagine how we would put up with someone like the gay people I'd seen on TV. I pictured him having sex with groups of men and wearing dresses, make-up, and making a fool of all of us. I didn't want to go see him because I didn't want to know if he was gay. It would be easier to push the thoughts out of my mind. After all, a man couldn't be gay and a father, could he? He would never have had sex with a woman if he was gay.

About eight months after he and his wife split up, Jim called and told me that he was gay. That was an awful day for me. I begged him to get some help and not to tell anyone else. I couldn't imagine how he could live with himself, and I knew that his sons would not want to have anything to do with him. And he had been such a good father. It didn't seem fair! At the same time, I was really angry with him. He had been married for a long time; surely he could have just kept on the way he was. I knew I would never be able to accept his coming for a visit with a male friend. It just seemed best if he would go away and not tell anyone. I was stunned when he told me that he planned to tell his sons.

Over the next few months he wrote me lots of letters, and I would call him often to see how he was doing. I begged him to reconsider, to see that he was throwing his life away, to not give up his children. Sometimes I was angry and hurt; other times I could see that he was still that same Jim I had loved all these years. I felt so alone and would never talk about it to anyone. All I could picture was that he was turning into some kind of faggy man, chasing other faggy men around, and possibly getting AIDS. Finally, he told me he had let his older brother know, so I had at least one person to call from time to time. Then his sons started calling me. They didn't like it any better than I did, and we would talk for hours about him. I could see their hurt and confusion, and I could understand why one of them would not talk to his father. The youngest was getting ready to graduate from college and was so afraid he would be embarrassed if Jim wanted to come to his graduation. Somehow all of us got through those days, but we sure did shed lots of tears. I once told Jim not to mention being gay around me. I could see the hurt in his eyes when I said that, and I felt so awful, but I just did not want to have to know about it. I kept hoping it would go away. At times I felt so guilty, wondering what I had done to make him into a homosexual. My husband died years ago, and I often would think that if I had remarried he would have had a man to model after. Now I understand that being homosexual is something that happens because of many influences. Perhaps our family played some role in it, but I also think that he was just born that way. He didn't choose it any more than we made him homosexual.

Looking back, I don't see how Jim got the courage up to change his life. He is so much happier today, and he wants all of us to be a part of his new world. I was so impressed when I met his friends. They were just like any other group of people, only most of them are lesbians or gay men. Sometimes I get uncomfortable with the way some of them express themselves, calling each other honey or darling and kissing each other around me, but they have been wonderful to me, and I can tell that the boys like them too.

At first, I thought that my other sons would have to take over being the father to Jim's boys. I just thought that a gay man would not want to be bothered with children. I pushed his sons to talk with their uncles and tried to make sure the boys didn't turn out gay. Once I began to relax—or maybe all of us began to relax—we learned that we could love each other just as before, and that being gay made a difference in Jim, but that lots of that difference was for the better.

Finding a chapter of P-FLAG (Parents and Friends of Lesbians and Gays) was a godsend for me. It was so helpful to be able to talk with other parents and to learn that my situation was not so strange. I will probably never be an activist, but I am not afraid to speak up when I hear people put lesbians and gays down. I still worry often about how Jim's boys will ever share their families with him. It will not be easy explaining to their wives and their children that their father is "different." Well, it's just a hard situation for everyone. Jim has so much to offer as a father and as a grandfather. I hope they will be able to work that out. I can't image how his grandchildren will ever explain him to their friends, but that's for them to solve.

At times it just doesn't seem fair; at other times I can see that Jim is teaching all of us some important things about loving people who are different, and I am grateful that we have such a fine person to learn from. I am proud when I see him working for his community, and I can't imagine where he gets the courage to admit that he is gay. I still have not told any of my friends. They would never understand. I wish it was not that way, but it's easier not to have to watch them avoid him or me because they are so set in their ways.

Sometimes I still have a hard time understanding how he can be gay and a father. The two just don't mesh. He tells me that he has met lots of other gay fathers, even some who arranged to have children knowing they are gay. I get mixed up when I think about those men and their children. "Those poor kids," I find myself thinking. "Who will teach them what men are like? How will they ever be able to feel good about themselves if their father is openly gay?" Then I realize that the important thing is for people to have parents who love them. Jim loves his sons and is determined to continue to be a part of their lives. Probably other gay fathers are a lot like Jim. If so, their kids are lucky.

I can tell that Jim respects us and does not put us in situations that might cause embarrassment. He's brought his lover home two or three times, and the two of them took the boys on a long trip last summer. They seem like a happy family. I guess we've all worked hard to adjust to this. The truth is that it is hard having a gay son or a gay father. But there are also some things we've learned that we wouldn't know otherwise. Even though I grew up with lots of prejudices, I no longer am so quick to reject people just because they belong to an "outside" group. People deserve respect and an opportunity to live their lives in the best way they can. If that means being gay, they should be treated just like anyone else. Some of the unfair things that have happened to Jim and his friends are so awful.

I still worry about AIDS, and there are days when I wish this had not happened to us. Jim is such a fine person, and if his sons turn out like him they will get along just fine. I hope they are not gay, but if they are, I will love them and support them like my other grandchildren. Maybe one day the world will change so that gay people don't have to be so afraid of how they will be treated. I hope that happens.

Parents and wives of gay fathers also have unique emotional responses upon learning that the man they have seen in one dimension is actually an entirely different individual. As their son or husband comes out to them, they too become involved in their own coming out process. Finding people to talk to within their current social support network, as well as entering new social support systems, is a typical response. One wife said:

> At first I was so ashamed. I knew there was no one I would be able to talk with about what had happened. I was also angry and wanted to blurt the news to everyone I knew. It was so easy to blame Mike for the breakup of our marriage, and if people knew he was gay, I would not be seen as part of the cause. But, as time passed, I realized that this man had been a good husband and a good father, and that our lives had about them a richness that was valued by both of us. Sure, he had betrayed me, but he had also stood beside me and loved me as best he could. Eventually I began to tell people—not everyone, of course. Some people seemed to understand, others got very uncomfortable and would change the subject. I learned that was their problem, not mine, and I no longer feel rejected by their inability to accept this part of me.

Although research on wives and parents of gay fathers is virtually nonexistent, anecdotal reports indicate that they share common concerns. Other than struggling with the coming out issue mentioned above, they also frequently report that they reexamine their own emotional responses to homosexuality, experience feelings of guilt about where they went wrong, become anxious about the impact on children and grandchildren, feel angry at their sons and husbands for creating this situation, and become distressed over the awkwardness involved in integrating their loved ones and gay friends into the family system. Today there is the added fear of the extent to which they or their loved one may be exposed to human immunodeficiency virus (HIV) (Robinson, Skeen & Walters, 1987). This latter issue will be discussed more fully in chapter 6. Let's examine wives and parents separately to determine the commonalities of their experience and ways the mental health professions can respond to them.

Coming Out to Parents

Parents of gay fathers often face a dual crisis. If they have been unaware of their son's homosexuality, they encounter the emotions surrounding that information at the same time they face their own emotional responses to the potential dissolution of his family. Anxieties about the way his life will unfold, combined with renegotiating their relationship with their daughter-in-law and concern for the well-being of their grandchildren, often leave these parents devastated and overwhelmed. The process begins when they learn their son is gay.

Fortunately, there has been significant research on the coming out process. Virtually every book on the topic of homosexuality addresses issues related to informing parents that one is gay. Parental responses fall along a continuum from total rejection to integration. Not unusual is one client's father's comment, "If you're gay, just don't come home again." That contrasts markedly with one mother's comment, "I've wondered if he was gay for years. It hurts me to think of the years he has struggled with this by himself. If only I had known, maybe I could have helped him not feel so alone and afraid. He is gay because he was born that way, and I admire his courage in living his life as the person he is." As is true about the adjustment to any change, accepting a son's homosexuality is a process that can take time.

Generally, both gay men and their parents report that the initial reaction is negative. For parents, the news that a son is gay often conflicts with negative sanctioning about homosexual activity, and they tend to see their sons' behavior as a choice. This is not surprising since "homosexuality refers to a type of behavior rather than a condition" and "homosexuals are viewed not just as people who do a certain type of thing, but rather as people who have a certain type of being" (Warren, 1980, p. 124). The son who had seemed so familiar suddenly appears as a stranger, and the parents encounter their own homophobia as well as their lack of knowledge about homosexuality. Embarrassed and ashamed, their attempts to encourage their son to abandon his gayness is often more connected to their own concerns about becoming stigmatized themselves. Their lack of knowledge renders them helpless as they attempt to find and construct a family role for a person who is homosexual.

Some homosexuals decide that telling their parents is not appropriate. Using the excuse that "it would just break their hearts," or "they're just too old to accept this," or "there's really no reason for them to know" cuts off parent and child from what can be both a painful and joyful aspect of their relationship. It also means that the homosexual will expend a certain amount of energy in keeping the secret, and excessive amounts of guilt might accumulate.

What Parents Say about Lesbian and Gay Children

Negative parental feelings are frequently followed with strong feelings of guilt and personal failure in their parenting roles (Weinberg, 1972; Jones, 1978). As they begin to examine themselves, a usual question they ask is, "Where did we fail?" While such feelings of blame are common, there is no basis for their legitimacy in the research literature (Jones, 1978; Hooker, 1969; Newcomb, 1985; Zugar, 1980). Homosexuality does not appear to result from an identified pattern of parenting. Further, there appears to be no connection between parenting of gay fathers and gay men who do not become fathers. Skeen and Robinson (1985) compared the early family backgrounds of thirty gay fathers with a matched national sample of gay nonfathers. No difference was found between gay fathers' and nonfathers' perceptions of parental acceptance, although both groups reported their mothers as more accepting than their fathers. Both groups also reported living in intact homes with heterosexual parents, retaining pleasant childhood memories where marital discord was uncommon. Basically, this study supports the notion that parents are not factors in laying the groundwork for the creation of gay families.

In their book reporting the parent experience with homo-

Box 5–1
STAGES OF PARENTAL GRIEF

As they respond over time to the knowledge that their children are gay, research suggests that parents travel through five stages of mourning and loss, in the following order: shock, denial, guilt, anger, and acceptance (Robinson, Skeen & Walters, 1987; Robinson, Walters & Skeen, 1989; Skeen, Walters & Robinson, 1988).

Shock. Parents said they were initially shocked when they discovered their child was homosexual. One mother said she was totally hysterical and spent two days in bed to recover. Feelings of disbelief and helplessness are also common. Their children had suddenly become strangers, and parents feared the dangers of homosexual lifestyles. They worried that their children would want to have a sex change operation, worried that their other children might also be gay, worried that they caused it, or worried because they didn't know anyone they could talk to. Other parents were simply concerned about covering up for their children to relatives, friends, and co-workers. Feelings of hurt, sadness, and depression often accompanied the shock or appeared as the shock wore off.

Denial. Once past the initial shock, parents typically tried to deny the reality that confronted them. They convinced themselves that this was just a phase their child was going through. "I thought it was not really true—that he would still meet someone from the opposite sex with whom he could have an intimate relationship," said one father. Another parent confessed, "I was unsure that it was so, or it was just something he was trying out—or copping out to."

Guilt. When the truth of their child's sexuality continued to confront parents, other emotions took over. "My feelings were intermixed and repeated over a period of two years," says a mother. "Because he asked us not to talk about it, it left us with a strand of hope for about a year. Then I knew I had to deal with it." Typical of most parents, this woman felt guilty and thought that she was to blame for her son's homosexuality. "All I could think about," she said, "was, Why us? What did we do wrong? I thought it was an illness caused by something I had done wrong or failed to do that I should have done." Other parents felt guilty for harboring certain attitudes, like the father who confessed, "I felt that early prejudices and remarks were coming back to haunt me—that it was payback time." Another mother said, "I felt a little guilty about some attitudes—especially ignorance that I had had about homosexuals."

Anger. Guilt and blame often naturally turned into anger directed toward self or spouse. "I was angry at my emotional reaction, angry at the pain it was causing my son," said one mother. The wife of a traveling salesman became furious with her husband for being away from home so much. "See what you have caused," she retaliated frequently. As parents became more informed about homosexuality, they learned that although its origins are unknown, they were not the cause and that it is possible for homosexual men and women to lead happy lives. Still, this increased awareness sometimes was coupled with anger. Said one parent, "I began to talk more and to inform myself, mostly through reading. I felt he had a need to flaunt it, which I felt wasn't necessary. I don't feel that way now—I rather understand his need to be who he is without fear." Looking back, she reminisced, "It has been about nine years since I found out. I remember expressing anger, and I think I did it more because I thought I was supposed to react that way. At least it was a way of releasing feelings, and I had to do *something,* I thought." Another parent was upset that her son didn't trust her: "I was angry that my child didn't tell me sooner. I felt he didn't trust me enough to know I wouldn't reject him. I didn't understand his fears and trauma about coming out."

Acceptance. The journey from shock to acceptance corresponds to those stages found among people mourning the death of a loved one. In a way, this period of several months to several years can be thought of as a grief process for the death of their child's heterosexual identity—an identity these parents maintained since their child's birth. One man said he grieved for his son. "I mourned him as if he had died," he remembers. "I felt like he *had* died, even though intellectually I knew he was alive." And one woman said she felt grief for her own dreams for her child. Many parents described acceptance as a Dr. Jekyll/Mr. Hyde change. "I was relieved to at last really know my son," said one woman. "At last he would be his true self. The invisible wall had finally disappeared. No more living two different lives—one for himself and one for the family he loves. Now we could *really* relate—no more quiet dark places." Another parent, although upset to know what caused her son's unusual behavior, was still relieved, "He told me on the phone, and when we finished talking and hung up, I cried and cried, and yet I was relieved to finally know for sure what was really wrong with him and what made him so depressed," she said.

Some parents became stalled in one stage of the mourning process and never completely worked through their reactions. "I felt like, and still do, that the joy has gone out of my life," confessed one mother. "I don't think I can ever be completely and totally happy again—not even for a moment." Some regressed on occasion to an earlier stage, like the father who said, "I still revert to denial," or the mother who said, "Denial, guilt, anger, and acceptance come and go from time to time, denial seldom and acceptance predominant."

---

sexual children, Griffin, Wirth & Wirth (1986) validate the findings of the professional literature. Acknowledging the reality of the parents' pain and sorrow, joy, freedom, and commitment, they report that parents are distressed with religious attacks on homosexuals, that they often take on the responsibility for their child's homosexuality, and that they do grieve the loss of grandchildren and status in their social networks. It is their loneliness that keeps them stuck, even though the movement to a positive viewpoint about homosexuality is not an easy one. Initially, the parents interviewed who were participants in Parents and Friends of Lesbians and Gays (P-FLAG) either broke off contact with their children, tried to convince them to change their sexual preference, ignored the issue, or attempted to accept the reality of the situation.

Learning offers the best means to progress, and information can be found in many sources. There are books that dispell many of the myths about homosexuality, other gay men and lesbians are available for dialogue, other parents of homosexuals can be met through participation in a support group like those offered by P-FLAG, ministers and other clerical people can be a valuable source of information but must be sought out carefully, and there are professionals who can be extremely helpful in alleviating the sense of alienation that is so typical.

Feelings typical among parents are grief, anger, sadness, guilt, failure, and shame early in the process (Robinson, Walters & Skeen, 1989). As parents confront their own homophobia and questions about their own sexuality, they must reformulate basic aspects of their world view. Acceptance can come as they move from self-centered concern to empathy about their son's situation. As they recommit to their son and become aware of his pain, needs, and wants, they begin to reintegrate him into their lives. This usually means including his lover and other gay friends and may require that they become comfortable with physical expressions of closeness between men. Surprisingly, many parents find this son a source of strength as they come to appreciate the courage with which he is living his life and as they develop a more honest relationship with him. They often experience feelings of renewed pride, an ability to laugh about their situation, letting go, comfort in the ongoing relationship, and mutual expressions of love and affection. At this point some parents begin to come out themselves, either with information to only the extended family and friends or as activists for gay rights causes.

Finally, these authors suggest that parents who find themselves absorbed with fear that their son will contract AIDS recognize that there is probably a connection between their feelings about this disease and the stigma attached to being homosexual. Magical thinking, such as, "My child will be protected" is not going to be helpful. Rather, parents need to gather facts about AIDS, discuss their concerns and share information with their son, devise an emergency plan in the event he does become infected, put their fears on hold and communicate their trust to their son. Finally, parents are advised that drawing from the time they came to accept their son's homosexuality, they focus on accepting that they cannot change everything in their world and that they will survive better by being aware of the positive aspects of the relationship they have with their son. Some parents do get involved as volunteers in local AIDS service organizations and may find themselves reassured as they learn more about HIV disease and the variety of ways individuals and their families respond to it.

The Process of Parental Adjustment

DeVine (1984) reports that parental reaction follows a five-step process. Each step has important issues demanding resolution, and not all families successfully move through all five steps; some become caught on one step indefinitely. According to DeVine, there is an initial time of *subliminal awareness* that their son or daughter is gay. These feelings are rarely discussed and often exist from observations over the years. At disclosure or discovery, the *impact* of the news that these suspicions are true creates a crisis as the parents exert pressure on the child to change to a heterosexual orientation and struggle with trying to keep this news secret. In this phase parents often feel alone and panicky.

The *adjustment* period comes as information is gathered and parents learn that their child continues to demonstrate those qualities previously prized. Respect returns and the family begins to build a role for this member who is "different." During the *resolution* period, parents mourn the loss of their child's heterosexual role and its implication in terms of a lost family structure (grandparenting, etc.) as well as changes in life, career, and social goals. As these losses are mourned, parents are also involved in dispelling the negative myth about the homosexual stereotype. Finally, there is a potential for *integration,* in which the new roles for all involved become more clearly defined and new behaviors come to be seen as a source of growth for the family as a whole. DeVine sees this process as being heavily influenced by the degree of cohesion or closeness in the relationship and the degree of flexibility in the regulative structures or rules and roles the family has created, and points out that family themes that define values and expected behaviors must be renegotiated. Families that succeed in the process of integrating a homosexual member are likely to be those that prize difference and encourage individual expression, that use power flexibly, and that are able to see crisis as an opportunity for growth, not just as dangerous. Those families with rigid rules and inflexible sex-role structures are likely to have a difficult time affirming a homosexual child (Storms, 1978).

Family themes often are presented in subtle ways. As parents struggle with a perception that their child can simply choose to be heterosexual, they are demonstrating a lack of knowledge about sexuality and homosexuality. Those who present feelings of shame and guilt may be actually struggling with ways to justify the incompatibility of their religious beliefs and homosexuality. Religion poses a unique challenge to these parents because often they have put great amounts of internal trust and social participation in religious institutions. Finding ways to affirm a child's homosexuality without abandoning what has been a major source of strength and meaning in their lives is an arduous, if not impossible, task for many.

Parents who learn to solve problems mutually are entering a time of changing their orientation toward both their own child and homosexuals in general. Those parents who can see that a homosexual lifestyle offers their child more than just a means of sexual expression are apt to move forward positively.

When the homosexual son is also a father, the parents are faced with a dual crisis. As their son's marriage is dissolving and he discloses information about his sexuality that seems both horrendous and incompatible with his father role, they often join with the daughter-in-law and grandchildren in rejecting this former heterosexual whose behavior seemed so predictable. The family as a whole is embarrassed and angry over what seems like an impossible situation. One mother wrote to her son, "I believe you are homosexual because you were born that way, but I don't see why you are choosing to be that now. Don't you love your children enough to keep on living the way you have for the past eighteen years?" A father said:

> I guess I can accept him as a homosexual but I just can't see why he would give up his family. Doesn't he know that they will not want him at their graduations and weddings and that he will never get to know his grandchildren? It seems like he expects all of us to just welcome him with open arms. It's just not going to be that way, especially since he obviously loves his boyfriends more than his children.

The reality is that having a gay son or father both adds and detracts from one's quality of life. There is a richness and diversity within the gay community that can become a source of tremendous satisfaction and enjoyment, and, of course, learning about any minority group can enable people to give up limiting prejudices. On the other hand, just like their sons and fathers, parents and children of gay men will encounter stigma and rejection. In fact, many families do overcome these hurdles and find an incredibly rich, honest, and loving relationship with their sons, and they may acquire gay friends. When the gay father relationship can also include their grandchildren, the family system as a whole is strengthened.

A final comment is necessary about the gay man who elects parenthood through adoption or by hiring a surrogate mother. Although not the norm, this form of fathering is an option that more and more gay men are choosing. Their parents, like the parents of any couple who choose such a means of having children, face a unique set of problems that require special attention. Often they struggle with their disapproval of their son's decision and may feel a particular burden as sole grandparents and as heterosexual models for their grandchildren. As courts become more open to approving adoptions by gay men, this option will become more available, and it is anticipated that some gay men will become fathers to children with HIV disease (Herscher, 1989). Never-married gay fathers have been virtually unstudied by researchers; what is known about them has been gathered through limited reports.

Wives of Gay Fathers

The anecdotal reports from wives of gay fathers and indirect reports gathered from the gay fathers themselves indicate that at disclosure, most wives experience feelings of alienation from their husbands. A period of shock characterized by a sense of not really knowing the man they have been so intimate with masks a deeper level of concern that they are not able to trust their own perceptions of people around them (Strommen, 1989). Often they feel they have failed as wives and that perhaps their sexuality is also in question. The major concern is similar to that of parents, "What did I do to cause him to become a homosexual?" Although there may initially be anger, lingering hostility and bitterness rarely endure (Bozett, 1981; Miller, 1979; Ross, 1983). As noted previously, conclusions drawn from this research must be tentative because they are by and large retrospective data gathered from the gay fathers themselves and may not be reliable.

Hatterer (1974) suggests that women who are married to gay men ignore the signals about their spouses' homosexuality as a way of staying in the maladaptive relationship that somehow meets their needs. These women play a deliberate but perhaps largely unconscious role in maintaining the facade of a traditional relationship. Many of the wives in another study are in highly dependent marital relationships that endure in spite of the obvious relationship deficiencies (Coleman, 1985). These women are afraid they would not be able to make it on their own and tend to focus on the positive aspects of their marriage, hoping that the unaddressed issues will disappear.

Gochros (1985) investigated the adjustment process of thirty-three women upon learning their husbands are gay. Their reactions are tied to the quality of the relationship, timing of disclosure, and the wives' attitudes toward homosexuality. As they struggle with shock, blame, and guilt, their general coping mechanisms either fail them or pull them through. For example, those wives who are able to sort out confusing emotions and integrate new information in their responses to their husbands are more likely to adjust positively. Like other researchers, Gochros reports that most of the marriages end in divorce.

Hays and Samuels (1989) reported on twenty-one women who were married to homosexual or bisexual men. The subjects in this study had anticipated a long-lasting monogamous relationship, and over half were separated, divorced, or reported themselves as being in transition following disclosure of their spouses' homosexuality. Three of the women in this study married with knowledge of their husbands' sexual orientation. Common in their reports is the period of grief that accompanied disclosure, feelings of anger and betrayal over not having guessed the truth, and being blocked in seeking social support by their fears of disapproval and rejection. This fear extended to their children and husbands. The three women in this study who were choosing to remain married to their homosexual husbands reported marriages characterized by good communication, knowledge of their husbands' sexual orientation, and an equal right to enter into sexual relationships outside the marriage.

One of the wives we interviewed stated:

> When Hal told me he was gay, I was absolutely stunned. I had thought he was having an affair with a woman because he was so reluctant to have sex with me. But I never thought he would be involved with men. I was ashamed and felt dirty and just wanted him to go away. I will never let him near my children again. He deceived me and does not deserve to be their father. I have never told any friend or family member what really happened between us. They wouldn't believe it and would probably not want to have anything to do with us after they knew the truth. I did rush to my doctor to have an AIDS test. So far I don't show any indication that I am infected, but I am afraid to get involved with anyone else. What kind of man would want me after knowing I was married to a queer and that I could have AIDS? When he said he wanted to see the kids, I just laughed and told him that they were gone from his life. If he tried to see them I would go to court and tell everyone about him. That shut him up for good.

Although such enduring anger and bitterness is not typically reported in the literature, some women do totally reject their husbands and use disclosure of homosexuality as a weapon in custody decisions. Major questions about the wives of gay fathers remain to be answered. Among them are:

- Why do women enter heterogeneous marriages (heterosexual women married to bisexual or homosexual men), and are there any special characteristics that differentiate these women from those who marry heterosexual men?

- How do wives' experiences of such marriages differ during each stage, beginning with courtship, from experiences of wives married to heterosexual men?

- Why do some women stay in heterogeneous marriages and others do not?

- How do wives and children deal with the experiences and problems of disclosure, social stigma, and homosexual activities of the husband/father?
- What special concerns do these mothers have for their children?
- Are there differences in wives' experiences of the marriage based on the information provided or withheld before marriage about the husbands' sexual orientation and activities?
- Do these wives experience major crises, and, if so, what factors precipitate them?
- To whom do they turn for help? (Hays & Samuels, 1989, p. 83)

It is clear that many women who have been married to gay and bisexual men have a difficult time finding validation and support for their experiences. In some cities, support groups are beginning to be formed to allow these women to come together and share their situations. But, by and large, these are isolated events, leaving most of these women alone. Likewise, there is scant literature for them to review that might help them gain perspective about their marriages. While most of them report they eventually adjust to their life circumstances, there are, no doubt, countless others who do not come forward for assistance, or who still remain in the dark about their husbands' homosexuality. One woman said, "I suspect that my husband is sexually involved with men, but if I bring it up, I'm afraid he will leave. I think I could live with this if I weren't so afraid I might get AIDS. I don't know what to do. We haven't had sex in months; maybe he will just leave me alone."

Fortunately, a recent major investigation by Gochros (1989) provides some tentative direction for the mental health professional. Following up on her 1984 study, Gochros expanded her sample to include 103 women in several U.S. cities. The women were recruited from various sources, including publicity in newspapers, television, and radio, and certainly are not representative of the general population. Largely white, middle class, and well educated, they nevertheless offer valuable information. These women are like women in heterosexual marriages. They live fairly traditional lives, and many of them stay with their husbands in spite of knowledge about their homosexuality. They report their relationships in positive terms, and by and large are gay-positive. Those who remain in the marriage do so because either they are uncertain about what to do or because they experience the relationship as mostly positive and have learned ways to cope with their spouses' gayness. This includes meeting other gay men and learning about the gay subculture.

Gochros suggests that disclosure is best handled in the context of a loving relationship and includes in its content the expression of commitment to the wife. The wives in her study that made the best adjustment to disclosure had husbands who stated their love for their wives and children and who clearly saw their homosexuality as creating a dilemma for the family as a whole. They informed their wives directly of their situation and displayed empathy, concern, and reassurance to their spouses. For the wives in Gochros's study, the process of adjustment to disclosure involved three distinct phases:

1. An initial period of shock involved impaired intellectual and social functioning and was managed by attempts to stay calm and avoid impulsive actions;

2. The interim period lasting from weeks to years, was dominated by confusion and anger;

3. Reintegration occurred once the family system adjusted to the change, found new resources, and learned new ways of defining individual needs and rights.

Disclosure creates a crisis for most wives, and the most helpful professional responses fall within the framework of crisis intervention. Throughout the process, both wives and children are struggling with the issue of stigmatization.

While many of the women in this study sought help from family, peers, religious organizations, and often from the mental health system, others isolated themselves and were extremely cautious about whom they informed. Unfortunately, their experience in getting help was much like that reported by gay men in that many of them found the professional sources to be uninformed and often insensitive. Most distressing were the mental health professionals who were punitive toward the wives and blamed them for the husband's problem. Some of the wives wished for mental health professionals who could endorse their staying married to a gay man as a viable alternative lifestyle. Even in cities as gay-positive as San Francisco, the quality of help available was frequently inadequate.

Tips for Practitioners

Practitioners who become involved with families of gay fathers will find their work enhanced as they conceptualize the emotional responses being presented as emanating from a complex set of relationships and emotional interactions that are based in both the nuclear and extended family. It is also essential that the emotional responses be attributed to more than the fact that a husband, son, and father is acknowledging his homosexuality. Suggestions are made in the hope that services to all family members will assist their successful integration of this change in the family constellation.

HELP FAMILY MEMBERS DEAL WITH SELF-BLAME

Feelings of blame will be tossed around by all family members. Parents tend to struggle with guilt over having turned their son into a homosexual by faulty parenting. Wives may report feeling their perceived sexual inadequacy drove their husbands to homosexuality. And the gay father, often feeling so totally responsible for the hurt and confusion he has created, may blame himself unfairly. The proper stance for the counselor is to provide information that will assist each person to understand that homosexuality is not caused by anyone and to support the gay father's courage as he becomes more honest about who he is. Rather than losing energy blaming oneself or others, a more productive task is to examine individual needs in light of this discovery and to help the family system find ways to offer mutual support. Helping them identify and confront their anger and fear and dealing with them in a constructive way is an important key in their healing.

PROVIDE INFORMATION, REFERRAL, AND
SUPPORT GROUPS

Practitioners can be of service to some families by knowing religious figures in their communities who can provide sympathetic assistance as families wrestle with the clash between their values and their sons' lifestyle. Being aware of other resources, both locally and nationally, such as support groups for wives and parents and literature that can help these individuals put their situation in better perspective, will also be helpful. The most useful process will involve steps that alleviate the isolation that parents and wives report. Many family members come to understand and accept gay fathers with the support of Parents and Friends of Lesbians and Gays (P-FLAG), which has chapters in every major city in the United States and the world. This organization provides emotional support and advice for parents and spouses who are struggling with a son's or husband's homosexuality.

HELP FAMILY MEMBERS DEMOLISH THEIR
HETEROSEXUAL EXPECTATIONS

It is highly unlikely that the gay son or husband will change his sexual orientation back to a heterosexual lifestyle. It takes family members about two years to work through their grief and fully accept the gay father's same-sex orientation—the same amount of time it takes to complete the grief process associated with a divorce or death of a family member.

Borhek (1983) suggests that the grieving process serves the essential purpose of burying the old heterosexual image and creating a new homosexual image of the gay father. Practitioners can use approaches similar to those used in grief counseling to help family members come to terms with their feelings of loss over the death of the gay father's heterosexual identity. They can help family members understand that the longer they cling to the long-held fantasies of marriage, family, and a heterosexual lifestyle, the longer the mourning process takes. Once parents are able to bury their heterosexual expectations and accept their son's homosexual identity, parent-child bonds are strengthened and mothers and fathers report feeling closer to their children than ever before (Skeen, Walters & Robinson, 1988).

Help Families Recreate Their Roles

By and large, reports indicate that disclosure is ultimately most helpful if it comes from the gay father in a context of a loving, ongoing relationship, and if there is reassurance of a continued commitment. One mother's comment is typical, "When he told me he was gay, I thought he was also telling me goodbye. It was such a relief to know that he wanted to try to find ways for us to have a different relationship." Helping families create a role for the gay father is essential. Rather than allowing him to disappear, parents and wives can offer reassurance that he has a place in the family and that they are determined to help him work that out. The system will need to change to accommodate his homosexuality and possibly his gay lover and friends. This is also a process that can take time but has the potential of being extremely rewarding to all.

The parent or ex-wife who initially rejected the gay father may seek help in re-establishing contact. Rather than having them wait around for the son or ex-husband to come to them, it will be helpful if they can begin to formulate an awareness of what they have to offer the relationship and what they need from it. Communicating these parameters to the gay father may enable him likewise to extend his trust back into a relationship with them.

Finally, there may be legitimate reasons for a gay father to not disclose his sexual orientation to his parents, former spouse, and children. In such cases, assistance will be rendered by helping him explore the negative and positive consequences of his decision. This is best accomplished in an atmosphere that is not biased toward disclosure. While there are obviously risks involved in nondisclosure (discovery, excessive guilt, etc.), there is no one way to handle the issue of coming out to family members.

References

Borhek, M. (1983). *Coming Out to Parents: A Survival Guide for Lesbians and Gay Men and Their Parents.* New York: The Pilgrim Press.

Bozett, F. W. (1981). Gay fathers: Evolution of the gay-father identity. *American Journal of Orthopsychiatry, 51,* 552–559.

Coleman, E. (1985). Integration of male bisexuality and marriage. *Journal of Homosexuality, 11*, 189–207.

DeVine, J. L. (1984). A systematic inspection of affectional preference orientation and the family of origin. *Journal of Social Work & Human Sexuality, 2*, 9–17.

Gochros, J. S. (1989). *When Husbands Come Out of the Closet*. New York: Harrington Park Press.

Gochros, J. S. (1985). Wives' reactions to learning that their husbands are bisexual. *Journal of Homosexuality, 11*, 101–103.

Griffin, C. W., Wirth, M. J. & Wirth, A. G. (1986). *Beyond Acceptance: Parents of Lesbians and Gays Talk about Their Experiences*. Englewood Cliffs, NJ: Prentice-Hall.

Hatterer, M. S. (1974). The problems of women married to homosexual men. *American Journal of Psychiatry, 131*, 275–278.

Hays, D. & Samuels, A. (1989). Heterosexual women's perceptions of their marriages to bisexual or homosexual men. *Journal of Homosexuality, 18*, 81–100.

Herscher, E. (1989, November 27). "AIDS Child with Two Lesbian Moms." *San Francisco Chronicle*, A8.

Hooker, E. (1969). Parental relations and male homosexuality in patient and nonpatient samples. *Journal of Consulting and Clinical Psychology, 33*, 140–142.

Jones, C. (1978). *Understanding Gay Relatives and Friends*. New York: Seabury Press.

Miller, B. (1979). Unpromised paternity: The life-styles of gay fathers. In M. Levine (ed.), *Gay Men*. New York: Harper & Row, 239–252.

Newcomb, M. D. (1985). The role of relative parent personality in the development of heterosexuals, homosexuals, and transvestites. *Archives of Sexual Behavior, 14*, 147–164.

Robinson, B., Skeen, P. & Walters, L. (1987, April). The AIDS epidemic hits home. *Psychology Today*, 48–52.

Robinson, B., Walters, L. & Skeen, P. (1989). Response of parents to learning that their child is homosexual and concern over AIDS: A national study. *Journal of Homosexuality, 18*, 59–80.

Ross, M. (1983). *The Married Homosexual Man*. Boston: Routledge & Kegan Paul.

Skeen, P. & Robinson, B. (1985). Gay fathers' and gay nonfathers' relationship with their parents. *The Journal of Sex Research, 21(1)*, 86–91.

Skeen, P., Walters, L. & Robinson, B. (1988). How parents of gays react to their children's homosexuality and to the threat of AIDS. *Journal of Psychosocial Nursing, 26*,7–10.

Storms, M. (1978). Attitudes towards homosexuality and femininity in men. *Journal of Homosexuality, 3*, 257–266.

Strommen, E. F. (1989). "You're a what?": Family member reactions to the disclosure of homosexuality. *Journal of Homosexuality, 18*, 37–58.

Warren, C. (1980). Homosexuality and stigma. In J. Marmor (ed.), *Homosexual Behavior.* New York: Basic Books, 123–141.

Weinberg, G. (1972). *Society and the Healthy Homosexual.* New York: Seabury Press.

Zugar, B. (1980). Homosexuality and parental guilt. *British Journal of Psychiatry, 137,* 55–57.

6

The Impact of AIDS on Gay Fathering

THERE has been no research published on the impact of HIV disease on gay fathers. What is known exists largely through isolated case studies presented at professional meetings or through personal correspondence. Therefore, this chapter will consist of a brief overview of infection manifestation and AIDS treatment, followed by a series of cases that will stand alone. Drawn from our clinical work with gay fathers, each case has been selected for the unique glimpse it offers into the lives of gay fathers who are facing HIV disease. Specific counseling approaches and information about HIV disease are offered elsewhere (Dilley, Pies & Helquist, 1989; McKusick, 1986). These cases are offered without commentary and in the hope that the reader will come to see the human dimensions of these issues. Rex tells us about his lover's children's clumsy attempts to come to terms with their father's death. Will is a married bisexual father who tries to explain himself to his wife and children. Sandy gave his daughter up for adoption years ago and struggles with wanting to get to know her before he dies. Steve has raised his son alone and searches desperately for a family to take him before he dies. Brad lives in the public eye and tries to keep his sexual identity and HIV disease a secret from his family and friends. These cases represent real people. Names and some details have been changed in order to protect their identity.

Infection Manifestations and Treatment

The AIDS virus attacks the immune system such that infected people are vulnerable to a host of rare life-threatening diseases. Although AIDS leads to the breakdown of the body's ability to fend off infections, it is not the primary cause of death. Sixty percent of people with AIDS die from *Pneumocystis carinii* pneumonia (PCP); the other major cause of death is Kaposi's sarcoma (KS) (Centers for Disease Control, 1986). Other symptoms include yeast infections (thrush), swollen lymph glands, persistent coughing, recurrent diarrhea, and unexplained weight loss. Individuals who test positive to the presence of AIDS antibodies but who have not had PCP or KS fall into two categories. Those diagnosed with AIDS related complex (ARC) present many of the opportunistic infections noted above; others who test positive but present no other symptoms are designated HIV positive. This group, the "worried well," present a particular threat because they are carriers of the virus while not showing any visible symptoms. The anxiety they experience is often quite intense (Faulstich, 1987), and in fact 10 to 20 percent of them eventually develop AIDS (Holland & Tross, 1985).

Symptoms may also appear in the central nervous system. Due to brain lesions and other difficulties, people with AIDS suffer from malaise, social withdrawal, lethargy, a reduced sex drive, confusion, and hallucinations (Faulstich, 1987; Holland & Tross, 1985). At times the confusion results in poor concentration. Some people with AIDS report that they have found themselves driving and unable to remember where they are going, have lost their cars in parking lots, or have gotten lost commuting to familiar places like the grocery store or church. Reactions to these symptoms range from severe alarm and fear to learning to deal with such events as inconvenient but not critical. One man said:

> Now I only drive to three places: my doctor's, the grocery, and church. Recently I started wearing an identification bracelet so if something happens to me my identity will be known. I keep a list of phone numbers in my wallet and just call someone if I

get lost. Sometimes the hallucinations are really bad, especially in the middle of the night. My friends put a little sign by my bed to remind me that what I am so frightened of is not real. I guess they got tired of me calling them scared out of my wits at two or three in the morning. Now when it happens, I read the sign and try to calm down and get back to sleep.

At this time there is no treatment that will restore the immune system. People with AIDS generally are prescribed azidothymidine (AZT), which apparently prevents further damage to the immune system. But even taking this drug creates difficulties. Beyond the temporary side effects, AZT is generally prescribed to be taken by mouth every four hours, making eight hours of uninterrupted sleep a thing of the past. Many people with AIDS complain that taking AZT forces them to be constantly aware of their illness, with this intrusion of AIDS into their sleep often seeming outrageous. Opportunistic infections (PCP and KS) are treated with traditional approaches, such as antibiotics, radiation, and chemotherapy, but these interventions have no impact on the AIDS virus. There is little hope that a vaccine for AIDS will be discovered until well into the 1990s or beyond the year 2000.

THE CASE OF OTIS: A GAY FATHER WITH AIDS, FROM HIS LOVER'S VIEWPOINT

Rex, twenty-eight years old, spoke with us three years after his lover, Otis, died of AIDS.

I was sixteen when I first started dating Otis, who was then forty-two. Otis was a federal narcotics agent. As he started experiencing his emerging homosexual feelings in 1975, the government found out and decided to get rid of him. They set him up in a pornographic bookstore, arrested him, and threatened to ruin his children's and wife's lives if he didn't resign. His wife found out about all this. Otis wanted to stay together, but his wife wouldn't agree to that. So Otis left his job, divorced his wife, and became a pharmacist. He walked out with nothing. He gave his wife everything they owned. When I met him,

it was his first Christmas; he had nothing but a fir tree deco-
rated with lights in an apartment he was renting.

I met him at a restaurant where I was a waiter. It was a very
busy restaurant in Seattle. He was a regular customer, and we
always watched each other out of the corners of our eyes. One
day I came through with a huge platter of food and had to
squeeze through a mass of people standing around drinking.
As I squeezed by him, face to face, I asked him if he'd like to
go out and he said, "Sure."

After we started living together the only time we'd ever see
his children (all three of them were in their twenties and thirties) was when they needed money. They'd come in asking for
thousands of dollars, and he would give them a check. They'd
say, "Thanks, Dad," and "Hi!" to me, and they were out the
door. At that time Otis tried to satisfy his children to get rid of
his guilt. He began to have financial problems because he was
giving them three and four thousand dollars at a time; checks
started bouncing because he was afraid that if he said "No,"
they'd reject him. But finally he told them "No more money,"
and they stopped coming around.

Of course, they had a lot of brainwashing from their
mother. She talked about her religious beliefs and harped
about how Otis had done them wrong and even said that he
was evil. They listened more to their mother than they did to
him. They didn't realize how much they loved their father until
it was too late. He wrote to his children even though for years
and years they never wrote back. It was like a one-way conversation. Once they married and had children and started thinking about Grandpa, they started calling him and corresponding
with him. Otis never heard "I love you" from his children until
two years before he died. Two of them started coming around,
but the third never forgave Otis for leaving the family and for
being gay.

After his children realized that Otis and I had a loving, enduring relationship, they started to take me more seriously. It
took seven years for them to get beyond the "Hi!" stage, but
finally his daughter started calling and writing me, too. She'd
ask, "Are you two really happy?" She was concerned that her
father was leading a happy life. We developed a great relationship by phone and mail even though we now lived three thousand miles apart. I think that gay fathers do pull away from
their children, too. They are investigating a whole new world

and a new part of themselves. I think instead of drowning themselves in the gay world, fathers should keep communication between both those worlds. I don't know why it can't be one world, but I don't think we'll ever live to see that!

When Otis was dying of AIDS, his three children flew in early on a Thursday morning. They hadn't seen him in seven years, but it took them a whole day in town to call us. Even though they had come a long way, it took them all day to get their heads together and decide, "Well, it's time to go see Dad." When they finally came to see him, Otis was bedridden and very weak. He had no appetite, was frail, and could barely speak. They kept thanking me again and again for how well I was taking care of him. But they never kissed or even touched their father the whole time. They were so worried about AIDS that they just stood at the other side of the room. After a while they did pull up closer and sat beside him, but they never reached out to hold his hand or to caress him. It seemed so very cold to me.

There was a lot of small talk, and then they wanted to know how long it would be before he died. It was like something clinical. They didn't express much feeling. After about an hour and a half, they said, "We gotta go." They said they might come back later in the day, but we never heard from them again. After he died I got an azalea with a note from the three of them thanking me for taking care of their father. When they finally had realized their father was a real person, it was too late. He was dying. I think they believed that Otis got sick with AIDS because of his "immorality." They might have been more compassionate if he had been dying of cancer or some other disease. It was real hard for them to accept that their father had AIDS.

Of course, even medical staff were nervous about AIDS back then in 1985. In the hospital there was a lot of phobia and hostility from the medical staff. The nurses wouldn't pick him up when he fell on the floor. They'd leave him in the shower for two or three hours, not wanting to help him get out. The care was just awful! It's hard to believe that human beings can be like that; it's like they wanted to persecute him because he had AIDS.

It was hard for me to realize that someone I loved so much was slipping through my hands. It made me a stronger person, but it was a tough time to go through. It was very exhausting, and it was a lot of work. Bringing him home from the hospital to die was like taking on another full-time job. He was a great man, very understanding, intelligent, and loving. I still go through my emotional times even though it's now been three years. I miss him dearly, and I always will.

THE CASE OF WILL: A BISEXUAL FATHER WITH AIDS

Will was forty-two when he was first interviewed. Although outwardly fairly healthy, he was thin, withdrawn, and wanted his life to come to a rapid end. He had married at twenty-two and was the father of two sons, twelve and fourteen years old. At the time of our interviews, he lived with his wife and his sons. His parents were deceased.

Looking back I can see that I have been bisexual all my life. A cousin and I started having sex together when we were kids. I didn't think about it too seriously because it seemed like what we were doing was natural and not too different from the circle jerks and playing around that my friends did. In high school I went out with the girls and had sex with my girlfriend for the first time when I was eighteen. From then on I mostly sought out females for sex. Later I got married without telling my wife about my playing around with men. I pretty much gave up having sex with men when my children were born. For a long time I just had sex with my wife.

But things changed after about nine years. Lonnie and I had not been getting along, and when a man I met in a motel bar while on a business trip suggested that we go to a gay bar, I quickly accepted. Once there, I felt an energy I had forgotten all about. Before the night was over, I had had sex with two men. Trying to figure all of this out after it happened was rough. I knew I liked having sex with my wife, but sex with men was also wonderful. I worried about it a lot and decided to try to keep my contacts with men to a minimum.

Usually I would only go out looking for a man when I was under a lot of stress, either at work or home. Over the years I learned about the bookstores, parks, and other public places where men have sex. I never knew the names of the men I had sex with. I didn't even ask their names because I knew I did not want to have an ongoing relationship. I was scared a lot about being found out, and I never told my wife anything about it.

Our sex life had trailed off over the years, and now I can see that we really lost touch with each other long ago.

I found out I had AIDS when I got so sick with a cold that I had to go to the hospital. At first, everyone seemed puzzled, but finally my doctor suggested an HIV test. I knew then I was in big trouble. As sick as I was, I tried to explain this thing I didn't really understand myself. Lonnie got real angry, and we both cried, but she didn't leave me. Once the doctor told me that I had PCP (*Pneumocystis carinii* pneumonia), I hoped I would die right there in the hospital. But I got better, and then my life became a real nightmare.

I have a very professional job that requires concentration and skill. I wasn't sure what to tell the people at work, so at first I just said I had pneumonia. Later as I began to get sicker, I told them I had leukemia. That's the same thing I told the kids and our friends. Lonnie told her parents the truth, and they got very angry with me. Of course, she was angry with me too. Fortunately she does not have the virus. I cannot believe I placed her at such risk. If both of us were to die, our children would really have a hard time. I think her parents and some of the medical staff really hate me for that. Sometimes I hate myself for it, too.

Last Thanksgiving Lonnie's parents called to tell me not to come for dinner since they were "sure I would get too tired from all the excitement." I knew just what they were really saying. They did not want me around any longer. Lonnie and the boys went without me, and I think that was one of the loneliest days I've ever spent.

After a while, Lonnie quit talking to me. She insisted that I move into the spare room downstairs where I would be more "comfortable." If I walked into her room and just sat on her bed, she would be up in a flash, changing the sheets and telling me to stay out. I don't want to stay downstairs away from the family, but I can't do anything about it. I can't drive any more, and I no longer want to visit her family and watch them worry about the dishes I use. All of them treat me like I am some kind of monster.

A few months ago I told my doctor to stop all treatment. Life just got to be not worth living any more. About the same time we were referred to a counselor who knew something about HIV disease. She was really a help to me, but my wife refused to go back. Pretty soon I was attending a weekly support group even though I was terrified they might find out who

I was and blab it all over town. Those guys taught me that I can feel okay about who I am even though I have AIDS. They and the counselor convinced me to tell my kids the truth, and I have even made some audiotapes, talking about my growing-up years and my sickness so the boys will have something from me to help them understand this when they are older.

The strange thing was that I began to feel better! Soon I was driving the car again, and I started back on AZT for a few months. I recently had my third bout of PCP, and I've decided that the fourth will be my last. My life is going nowhere. My kids are the only ones who come in and talk to me each day. I spend most of my time in bed and alone, and I know this is about the best it is going to be. I've gotten information from the Hemlock Society about ways to kill myself, but I'm not sure I have the guts to do that. I get so depressed and just want to die.

Will died three weeks following our last interview. He had another bout of PCP and was too weak to fight it off.

THE CASE OF SANDY: AN AIDS-INFECTED FATHER WHO GAVE UP HIS DAUGHTER

Sandy is a forty-three-year-old man who lives on the west coast. He left his home in South Carolina shortly after his divorce. He continues to work in spite of his AIDS diagnosis.

I knew throughout high school that I was queer. I could feel the sexual attraction to boys and actually did start having sex with a friend of mine when I was eighteen. Feeling guilty about it, I went to my minister and confessed. I tried to explain myself as clearly as I could, and he seemed to be listening. When I got through he was quiet for a while and then said, "You are not homosexual. You are just going through a phase, and God has told you to give it up. What he wants you to do is to get married and have some children. These feelings will go away."

That's just what I tried to do. I gave up sex with men, got married the next year, and was a father just after my twentieth birthday. God knows how hard I tried to turn off the sexual feelings toward men. I loved my daughter, Amy, and my wife, and I didn't want to hurt them. But I could see that the situation was impossible. I knew that I would soon be unable to control my sexual attraction to men.

When I told my wife what was happening, she asked me to leave, and I did. Later, I was not surprised when she filed for divorce. After about two years she got married again. Even though I had not heard from her in a long time, she called me and asked me to let her new husband adopt my daughter. I didn't like it at first, but I got to thinking that she was not going to allow me to see her anyway, and realized it might be easier for Amy if she had the same last name as the rest of her family. So I signed the papers and moved away. I haven't seen her in seventeen years.

I've pretty much drifted around the country since. I can make good money in restaurants so I'm pretty free. I haven't been back home in over five years. They don't want me there, and it's just easier if I stay away. I talk to my mother on the phone from time to time, but I wouldn't say we're close.

I found out I had AIDS about six months ago. Actually it was not a surprise because I knew I had done just about everything and that I was bound to get it sooner or later. My lover is sick too, and we're trying to take care of each other, but we're both real scared. I don't know what we'll do when neither of us can work anymore.

I decided not to tell my family about my AIDS diagnosis. They can't do anything anyway, and I'm sure they would never let me come home to die. I'll just handle this on my own.

The other day my mother called to tell me that Amy had come around asking questions about me. I told Mom not to tell her I am gay and definitely not to tell her where I live. There's nothing good I can do for her now. She's better off not knowing these things about me. She'd probably be real ashamed to have to tell her friends that her gay father is dying from AIDS.

I would like to see her though. I asked Mom to send me her picture. When it came I was so surprised to see a woman who looks almost exactly like me! I've learned that she has done well in school and will go to college next fall. I don't take credit for those things of course; her mother and stepfather did that work with her.

I can't decide what to do about her when I die. I know I don't want to have her be here with me even if she wanted to come. I would like to leave her a letter or something so she will know that I only gave her up because I thought it would be best for her. I love her even though I don't know her, and I don't want to do anything that would hurt her or her future.

THE CASE OF STEVE: A CUSTODIAL, SINGLE-PARENT GAY FATHER WITH AIDS

When we interviewed Steve, he was very sick. Emaciated and weak, he had recently learned that the vision problems he had been having for several months were related to AIDS. He knew that he was slowly going blind. Steve lived with his lover, Ray, and his seventeen-year-old son, Paul.

Being Paul's father has been the most important part of my life. I married his mother because she needed a way to stay in this country. I told her I would marry her if she would let me have the child I hoped would come. We never lived together much, and she did hand Paul over to me not too long after he was born. I had him by myself for four years, and then Ray moved in, and Paul has had two "daddies" ever since. We told him as soon as he could understand that we were different from other families, and he's handled that really well. We've talked a lot about homosexuality. Paul says he is only attracted to girls, and he dates a lot, just like all boys his age.

Things have gone pretty well for us, at least until I got sick. Paul's mother has developed a major drug problem and has been in and out of drug treatment programs. We haven't seen her in almost four years now and don't even know where she is. When I first got sick, I tried to convince myself that I would be able to hold on until Paul was out of college. At first, I didn't tell him what the problem really was. I made up something about a skin rash and a "bug" that upset my stomach. He seemed to accept that, and our lives went on pretty much as before. Once I couldn't work any longer though, I knew I had to get things ready.

I sat down with Paul and told him the truth, that I have AIDS and that I am going to die. We both cried buckets that day. I had decided that we would find him a new family to take care of him after I died. Ray had gotten along with Paul just fine, but he did not want that responsibility, and I wanted both of them to be happy and free after I die. Paul resisted at first, saying that he would stay here and take care of me. But I pressured him, and finally he came around. We made a project out of gathering information and visiting our "prospects." My family had not had anything to do with me for years and had always thought that Paul was just one big mistake. They refused to acknowledge him as their grandchild. So they never made it on the list.

Paul went to Italy to visit his mother's family for three months. As much as I had hoped that would work out, it was just not the place for him. We had worked on the language, but he never really mastered Italian. And they didn't ever warm up to him. After a couple of months they sent him back to me. We tried a couple of other families before I remembered a distant cousin who lived in Australia. I talked with her a long time on the phone and had her fly over to meet with us. She lived alone and had always wanted children. Paul hit it off with her right away and ended up going back to visit for three weeks. When he came home I could tell that he was happy, and we were both relieved when she wrote asking him to come and live with her!

I have convinced Paul to go on and move before I die. I will feel a lot better knowing that he is happy and secure. It would be hard for me to die not knowing he was okay. Besides, this way he won't have to see me when I'm sicker. He will have a memory of me looking halfway decent. I don't know how I will ever be able to let him go. Knowing I will never see him again is the worst part. We're trying to find a way to say goodbye to each other. So far, I don't have any good ideas. I've signed all the papers so she can legally adopt him, so right now he's more hers than mine. That seems very strange to me. All of his life I've taken care of him. Now I've got to let him go.

Six weeks after this interview Steve took his life with an overdose of drugs. He had become blind and could no longer take care of himself during the day. Paul had gone to Australia the week before and did not return for the funeral.

THE CASE OF BRAD: THE ESTABLISHMENT GAY FATHER WITH AIDS

Brad, a fifty-two-year-old widower, had defined himself as gay for years. He never came out to anyone, preferring the safe anonymity of clandestine meetings in parks with men he did not know. His wife had died ten years ago, about the time that his four kids were leaving home. His children and grandchildren are an important part of his life, and he also values the social status he has worked hard to achieve in his small Southern community. He "dates" a divorcee in order to fulfill his social obligations in a manner that does not arouse suspicion. Still on the sly, he has had a sexual relationship with a thirty-

five-year-old man in the next town for the past two years. Brad learned recently that he has been infected with HIV.

I am in an absolute panic. My doctor tells me that I'm healthy and that I could go for years without having symptoms. But I notice every little bump on my skin, or every time I cough I think I have that pneumonia. I have had no one to talk about this with. I am so ashamed of myself and shudder to think what people will say about me when I do get sick. I've thought about just saying I have cancer, but some of my best friends are doctors and they would ask me questions I couldn't answer. Imagine what Kay (my girlfriend) will think once she knows. Fortunately, we never had sex. I was too afraid that I might give her something, and besides, I was no longer interested in having sex with women. I made up a story that I had a very low sex drive and basically found myself no longer interested in sex. She never has pressed me about it, but I can see that she is more than a little puzzled.

I finally talked with my boyfriend about what was going on. At first I thought he had given the virus to me, but it turned out that he was negative, so I guess I got it somewhere else. He tells me to sell my business, and he will come with me wherever I want to go. He thinks we can just leave everything behind.

I'm simply not willing to give up my children and my grandchildren. Last week, my four-year-old grandson spent the weekend with me. I had a great time taking him to the zoo and to the movies. Kay spent some time with us, but most of the time we hung around together. If my son even thought I had AIDS, he would probably not let me be around my grandson.

I've also thought about suicide when I begin to get sick. That's not the kind of thing I think I could do, but I also can't imagine what people will think of me when this gets out. They'll be talking about me for years, and even my friends will probably not want to have anything to do with me. I don't know what to do.

The other night at a dinner party someone was talking about how all the gays are getting AIDS. Kay told everyone that she thought they deserved whatever they got. Now what do you think she'll say when she finds out that her "boyfriend" is queer and has AIDS?

My counselor told me that maybe I should think about telling my children. He thinks they probably suspect that I am gay. Once when Tom (my boyfriend) was leaving, my daughter caught me kissing him goodnight. She just walked right out of the room and nothing was ever said. I'm sure she told the others, but nobody has said anything to me. I suppose one of these days I'll have to tell them. God, I feel so bad about ruining their lives. They'll never get over this.

It also makes a mockery of my marriage. I valued the years we spent together. We had a great family life, traveling and watching our kids grow up. I still miss her. If she had lived, I probably wouldn't be in this mess. When she was around I behaved myself pretty well. I don't know what to do!

I thought about trying to do it in stages. First I would tell everyone that I was gay, and at least that would be over. But who would associate with me if they knew that about me? I don't know any gay people other than my boyfriend, and it's too late for me to start all that anyway. But if I could do it that way, they would have time to adjust to my being gay, and then later I could tell them about AIDS.

I think people suspect that something is wrong with me. I've gained twenty pounds in the past six months. Just about all I do is sit around the house by myself and eat! I feel so safe at home alone, and I find myself turning down invitations for the first time in my life.

God, what am I going to do?

The Impact of AIDS

The impact of AIDS on the gay culture has been immense. In cities where there are large gay populations, it is not uncommon for people to report that they have seen their entire social network disappear because of AIDS. And these are the "easy" days of the AIDS crisis (Barret, 1989); as years go by more and more people will be impacted by the virus that causes AIDS.

The psychological needs of people with HIV disease are not unlike those of others who face a terminal illness. What is different, though, is that having HIV disease means encountering the stigma that Rex and others talked about. Although the situation regarding AIDS hysteria seems to be getting better, a person with HIV disease, his family, friends, and caregivers often find people avoiding them. Sometimes the person with AIDS even comes to view his own body as "dirty," an example of internalized stigmatization. It is also significant that most of the people who die from HIV disease are young men in their twenties, thirties, and forties. As these men struggle to make sense of their truncated lives, they frequently find themselves giving up their hard-won material possessions in order to qualify for federal and local assistance programs that pay their medical costs.

The emotional atmosphere that surrounds HIV disease is evident from the moment a person considers being tested (Martin, 1989). Emotions such as fear, anger, shame, confusion, depression, and guilt are commonly reported by those who are considering being tested as well as by those who know they are facing a deteriorating immune system (Barret, 1989). These emotions also are evident throughout the infected person's support system. Parents (Robinson, Walters & Skeen, 1989) and lovers (Geis, Fuller & Rush, 1986) also report struggling with these often overwhelming emotions. (See Box 6–1 for parental reactions to the AIDS epidemic.)

Box 6–1
WHEN AIDS HITS HOME: RESULTS OF A NATIONAL SURVEY

"I feel very good that I supported my son for being himself all during his life. That has made his death much easier to accept. He enriched the lives of most everyone who would allow it. When he died from AIDS, I felt my heart was broken, and I fell completely apart. I asked so much from my son, but from the onset I took care of him twenty-four hours a day, for sixteen months at home and two weeks in the hospital until his death. A great part of our life has gone, and I still hurt. I lost a wonderful son and a friend. My husband doesn't like to talk about my son, and I can't stop thinking about him twenty-four hours a day. I can't sleep—everything reminds me of how much he suffered."

This mother is one of a growing number of parents whose children have died from AIDS. A national study of over 700 parents of homosexual children found that they are having adjustment problems because they are either losing their children or are threatened with their child's death on a regular basis (Robinson, Walters & Skeen, 1989). Even in homes where there has been no AIDS diagnosis, fear dominated parents' thoughts. The outbreak of AIDS reopened old wounds for 90 percent of the parents who had come to accept their child's homosexuality. They reported a resurgence of fear surrounding their child's sexual orientation, and some confessed that they even wished their children were heterosexual because of the spread of AIDS.

Fully 71 percent of parents surveyed said they worried that their children might contract AIDS, and 78 percent said that they even worried about the health conditions of their children's sexual partners. Although they did not fear catching AIDS from their children, parents did worry that their offspring might suffer from the backlash of AIDS. Although 58 percent of parents believed that media coverage on AIDS had presented a balanced attitude, 80 percent felt that more media coverage on AIDS is needed, and 93 percent believed that more money for AIDS research is needed.

Despite all the fears and apprehensions, 89 percent of the parents insisted that the AIDS outbreak had not made them feel more negatively about homosexuals in general. Those who said that their attitudes had changed usually mentioned their strengthened opposition to sexual promiscuity and increased endorsement of "safe sex." One mother specifically said that her attitude had certainly changed toward "those who behave irresponsibly and continue to practice sex without proper precautions." An impressive 40 percent said they felt more compassion and concern for gay men as a result of the AIDS outbreak. "My sympathy for AIDS patients has increased as I have listened to and met personally some of them and their families," one parent said. "I see it as a human tragedy, not limited to gay[s]." A strong majority gave supportive answers to the question about AIDS and said if their sons contracted the virus they would support them to the fullest. One parent summed up the feelings of many: "I feel more compassion for the men that are dying. It could be my child. I hope that the media don't just show the negative side but educate that these are human beings, as are we all."

Tips for Practitioners

In the not too distant future it will not be unusual for gay fathers, their wives, ex-wives, and children to be calling on mental health professionals for assistance. Now is the time to begin learning about the emotional consequences of HIV disease. The mental health profession can play a positive role in helping local communities respond to this crisis in reasoned ways. Now is the time to begin learning about the psychological responses to HIV disease.

CONFRONT YOUR OWN DISCOMFORTS

A recent survey of practitioners in a major metropolitan city revealed that not one person in private practice would admit to having counseled an AIDS patient for fear of being stigmatized. Obviously, practitioners need to get their feelings clear not only about homosexuality but also about the HIV disease.

Providing services to people with AIDS places the practitioner in situations that can generate significant levels of discomfort. Being in contact with sick people (fear of infection), becoming comfortable interacting with homosexuals (homophobia), and being able to confront the issues that attend a terminal illness (fear of dying) are among the strongest emotional challenges that must be addressed prior to becoming involved. Discussions with family members, friends, and possibly employers about the consequences of becoming a part of a professional group that many view as "at risk" is one step in getting ready to serve in the AIDS community. Conversing with medical personnel about the true risk of contact with a person with AIDS and educating families and other groups about AIDS may be essential in order to maintain the kind of social support that working with terminally ill clients demands. Examining personal attitudes about death and assessing readiness about entering a helping relationship that probably will be permeated with feelings of helplessness and grief are also important steps.

GET YOUR FACTS STRAIGHT

Practitioners are in an ideal position to influence the way local communities respond to the incidence of AIDS. By learning about the disease and by becoming involved in providing assistance to those who have been diagnosed, professionals can play an important role in helping the general public separate the facts from the myths. Whereas not all practitioners will be comfortable providing direct service to people with AIDS, many are needed as AIDS educators or as fund-raisers for local AIDS organizations.

It is important to know the facts about AIDS to dissolve myths that set up barriers between practitioners and clients. This information is important to help practitioners pave an open communication system with clients as well as to impart information to family members who are often confused and misinformed about HIV disease. Being comfortable interacting with gay men and discussing their sexual activities is essential. You must know, for example, what "safe sex" is in order to hold such discussions with clients and their families.

There is a myth that working with terminally ill people is a highly charged, emotionally fulfilling and dramatic experience. Although this is often true, the more typical exposure is to extremely demanding situations and clients whose anger and helplessness create counselor frustration rather than empathy. Learning to confront counselor-directed anger because "You don't know what it's like to have AIDS" or "You don't know what it's like to be gay (or hooked on drugs)" or "You don't have to struggle like I do with being alone" is likewise essential. Being able to maintain a commitment to people obsessed with the negative aspects of a terminal illness is also an important skill. Abandoning people because the interactions are often extremely difficult will only add to their distress.

DEFINE YOUR LIMITS

The needs of people with AIDS can be overwhelming to the practitioner. Often the line between professional and human roles becomes clouded. Figuring out how often to visit a hospitalized patient who has no family and few friends can become quite complicated. At times you may need to resist the urge to provide money for medical care. At other times, you may not hesitate to provide food for a patient who has no money and was too weak to shop for himself. Practitioners must keep a close eye on dependence issues since it is easy to become trapped in a highly dependent and exhausting relationship.

ADDRESS ETHICAL ISSUES

There are many horror stories in which gay fathers have not told their wives of their sexual behavior and have infected them as well. Some experienced counselors of HIV seropositive gay men suggest that many of these men continue to engage in "at risk" sexual practices, endangering themselves and spreading HIV to others (Barret, 1987; Kegeles, 1988). The ethical dilemmas created when this behavior is explored are numerous and may generate sufficient anxiety for practitioners and other health-care workers. (See, for example, Gray & Harding, 1988; Kain, 1988; and Melton & Gray, 1988.) There are no easy answers for the ethical situations that will be faced. What to do about gay fathers with AIDS who are still active in anonymous sex and how to advise the father with AIDS who is not getting proper medical advice are common problems. We believe it is important to declare your own values about the ethical dilemma but to continue to provide counseling. Convincing seropositive gay fathers to inform their sex partners of their HIV status is critical and can be an ongoing theme in the counseling relationship. Getting this point across as well as convincing men to practice "safe sex" requires much creativity and persistence (Coates, Morin & McKusick, 1988; Hostetler, 1988; Krajick, 1988).

IDENTIFY AND ISOLATE THE "TRIPLE WHAMMY"

It is important to remember that in AIDS cases, gay fathers suddenly may be hurled into a three-pronged dilemma: being a father, being gay, and having AIDS. The HIV-positive diagnosis and the progression of the disease demand that these men disclose their homosexuality to spouses, children, and other family members who may have to deal with all these overwhelming issues at once. Families dealing with the "triple whammy" may need more intensive help than other gay father families.

Practitioners must help families untangle these issues so that they can deal with them in a healthy and productive way. Unresolved issues related to the father's homosexuality and his fatherhood status also may surface for the first time because of the AIDS crisis.

HELP GAY FATHERS SEE THE PITFALLS OF
BECOMING A DISNEYLAND DAD

Many men, straight or gay, who are separated from their children and see them only rarely often lavish gifts, trips, and material possessions on their kids to assuage their own guilt and to persuade the children to love them. This behavior has been labeled the "Disneyland dad syndrome" (Shepard & Goldman, 1979). Fearful of losing his children's love, the divorced gay father tries to win their affection through overindulgence rather than through a meaningful relationship. The focus of the interactions with his children is on material gifts and entertainment rather than expression of a natural, meaningful relationship. The important, daily things are missing—having time alone with his children in the evening, putting the children to bed, helping them with homework or to solve some personal problems, or cooking a meal together. So partly out of guilt and partly out of trying to cram months of time into a day, the visiting father overindulges his children with material comforts, which is also an insurance policy that he will not lose his children altogether. Some single fathers feel pressured to perform, to spend money, or to entertain their children so that they will want to see them again.

In the case of Otis, Rex told how this syndrome can even apply to grown children when Otis went bankrupt trying to relieve his own guilt over his homosexuality and to get his children to love him. The Disneyland dad syndrome can sabotage the father-child relationship. Children begin to expect material items and may harbor anger that their father cannot give them the most inexpensive gift of all: love. As they begin to see their children take and take, fathers too become bitter and resent the fact that an enduring and meaningful relationship has been replaced by superficial and conspicuous consumption. Practitioners can help gay fathers see the pitfalls in such materialistic relationships and help them carve the type of loving and meaningful relationships that will sustain themselves.

A THERAPIST SPEAKS ABOUT HIV DISEASE

I started working with people with HIV disease after several years of volunteer work with cancer patients and their families.

I am often asked questions like, "Doesn't your work depress you?" and "Aren't you afraid that straight people will avoid your practice if they know you work with people with AIDS?" My answers to those questions are simple: Yes and no. The work is quite difficult at times, and I have been afraid. I have watched people that I have come to admire and love slowly waste away. I have sat with their survivors as they grapple with issues of suicide and loss. And I have been inspired by numerous acts of courage and strength as young men face situations with a dignity they never dreamed possible. I tell each client in my practice that I work with people with HIV disease, and so far no one has walked out of my office for that reason.

Challenges abound in providing mental health services to people with HIV disease. The traditional psychotherapy model I learned in graduate school simply did not prepare me for the demands of this work. People with HIV disease often are unable to come to the office for their weekly appointments, and I have learned to make house calls and hospital visits. People with AIDS often find themselves near the brink of financial ruin, and I have continued to see many clients for no pay in spite of the enormous amounts of time some of them require. And my role often fluctuates as their health declines. For example, some may need me to assist them to buy groceries or even to help them pay for medical services they cannot afford. And I have gone to visit one man twice each day to feed him his breakfast and dinner as he slowly died alone in the hospital. I have even helped plan the details of funerals in cases where families abandoned patients. Finding the line between my role as a professional and my role as a fellow human being is always tough. There are no guidelines, no easy answers, and few colleagues to help the professional mark the bounds of the relationship. It is a task that must be worked out individually with one eye on the goal of helping and the other on the counselor's personal limits. I continually ask myself, "What is it I have to give to this situation without compromising my personal life too much?"

The differences from working with cancer patients abound. First, most of my HIV clients are young men whose lives have been seriously limited by this mysterious illness. At a time when they had anticipated becoming more secure financially and socially, they are giving up their careers and sometimes watching their friends disappear. For many, this happens without the comfort of family support. There is the stigma attached to HIV disease and the "hook" it often presents to unresolved issues related to the client's homosexuality. There is, of course, potential stigma for the counselor whose support system may not tolerate involvement with "infected" people who are also homosexuals. Both the stigma of HIV disease and homosexuality must be anticipated because both are real. Another difference is that many people with HIV disease are better informed about treatment than their physicians. I watched helplessly as one client slowly deteriorated from what was obviously HIV disease that had been misdiagnosed by his physician as Epstein-Barr mononucleosis. I worried about the appropriateness of providing the money to pay for the second opinion that ultimately rendered proper diagnosis and treatment.

There is also the constant uncertainty that surrounds HIV disease. There are many experimental treatments, some with severe side effects and with unknown outcomes. The patient must expend considerable energy researching treatments and their side effects. Counselors will learn about these treatments from their clients. HIV disease is rarely predictable. People can be near death one day and driving around the city a couple of days later. There are a lot of false alarms as well as genuine alarms with HIV disease.

There are also many ethical issues the counselor will face. Some people with HIV disease are reluctant to disclose their status to their sexual partners. Although stating that they are practicing safer sex, in fact some continue to engage in unsafe sexual activity, placing others, as well as themselves, at risk. For the wives and unborn children of gay fathers, this poses an especially complicated situation.

Thoughts of suicide are common, and I have learned how to assist those who want information about nonviolent ways to end their lives. And I have learned how to support the client's need to control his life to the extent of ending it if the quality of life remaining is intolerable. By and large, the mental health profession has been slow to respond to the AIDS crisis, leaving the practitioners who are on the line without adequate guidelines and support. The work is often quite lonely.

Conversely, working with people with HIV disease has been the richest of my professional experiences. I have come to know and love many fine people whose character and courage have inspired me. On the whole, the work has an integrity that is uncommon. As sick individuals, their friends, families, and medical support systems encounter this terminal illness, a pervasive honesty and dedication is evident. The kinds of issues that must be faced are far different from those presented by a person who is "vaguely unhappy" or faces a career change. Through this work, I frequently feel connected to the broader struggle for human rights for all people. It provides a perspective that enables me to renew my efforts when I am tired and burned out. I am continually touched and amazed by the spirit, dedication, and love that surrounds so many people with HIV disease. People can be transformed as they face this crisis, discovering in themselves previously unknown qualities that shape their lives in profound ways. There is also the excitement of working on a "growing edge" in the profession. What I am learning from my clients will be passed on to others so that they can perform quality work sooner.

I recently moved from North Carolina to San Francisco to further my understanding of the psychosocial aspects of HIV disease. It is often difficult to see the numbers of very sick people in this city. Of the 7,500 who have been diagnosed in San Francisco, over 5,000 have died. The gay community as a whole is shell shocked by massive, ongoing loss. Yet people continue to live their lives with courage, determination, and love as they anticipate the day when HIV will no longer be a life-threatening disease. Let's hope that day is not too far off, and let's work together to help those whose lives are endangered and who offer themselves as subjects in the studies that eventually will lead to a break-through.

What is ahead in terms of numbers of sick and dying people will test our medical system and our commitment to human rights. Now is the time for others to come forward and lend their support by learning how to provide services to people with HIV disease.

Bob Barret
San Francisco
January 2, 1990

References

Barret, R. L. (1989). Counseling gay men with AIDS: Human dimensions. *Journal of Counseling and Development, 67*, 573–575.

Barret, R. L. (June 1987). "Reducing Unsafe Sexual Practices of HIV Seropositive Gay Men: Education, Counseling, and the Twelve Steps." Paper presented at the Fourth International AIDS Conference, Stockholm, Sweden.

Centers for Disease Control. (1986). Update: Acquired immunodeficiency syndrome—United States. *MMWR, 35,* 17–21.

Coates, T. J., Morin, S. & McKusick, L. (1987). Behavioral consequences of AIDS antibody testing among gay men. *Journal of the American Medical Association, 258,* 1989.

Dilley, J., Pies, C. & Helquist, M. (1989). *Face to Face: A Guide to AIDS Counseling.* San Francisco: AIDS Health Project.

Faulstich, M. E. (1987). Psychiatric aspects of AIDS. *American Journal of Psychiatry, 144,* 551–556.

Geis, S., Fuller, R. & Lippman, S. (1986). Lovers of AIDS victims: Psychosocial stresses and counseling needs. *Death Studies, 10,* 43–53.

Gray, L. A. & Harding, A. K. (1988). Confidentiality limits with clients who have the AIDS virus. *Journal of Counseling and Development, 66,* 219–223.

Holland, J. C. & Tross, S. (1985). The psychosocial and neuropsychiatric sequelae of the acquired immunodeficiency syndrome and related disorders. *Annals of Internal Medicine, 103,* 760–764.

Hostetler, A. J. (1988). Secrecy about AIDS diagnosis: A sign of stigma, not a cause to legislate behavior. *The APA Monitor, 19,* 28.

Kain, C. D. (1988). To break or not to break. That is the question. *Journal of Counseling and Development, 66,* 224–225.

Kegeles, S. (1988). Intentions to communicate positive HIV antibody status to sex partners. *Journal of the American Medical Association, 259,* 216–217.

Krajick, K. (1988). Private passions and public health. *Psychology Today, 22,* 50.

McKusick, L. (1986). *What to Do about AIDS: Physicians and Mental Health Professionals Discuss the Issues.* Berkeley: University of California Press.

Martin, D. J. (1989). Human immunodeficiency virus infection and the gay community: Counseling and clinical issues. *Journal of Counseling and Development, 68(1),* 67–72.

Melton, G. G. & Gray, J. N. (1988). Ethical dilemmas in AIDS research: Individual privacy and public health. *American Psychologist, 43,* 60–64.

Robinson, B., Walters, L. & Skeen, P. (1989). Response of parents to learning their child is homosexual and concern over AIDS: A national study. *Journal of Homosexuality, 18,* 59–81.

Shepard, M. & Goldman, G. (1979). *Divorced Dads: A Practical Plan with Seven Basic Guidelines.* Radnor, PA: Chilton Book Company.

7

Problems in Studying Gay Fathers

THE CASE OF MICHAEL

Six months after my wife and I separated, I began to live to-gether with Hunter, my first male partner in a committed rela-tionship. He was very fond of my five-year-old son and en-joyed caring for him. He frequently read him bedtime stories and helped in caring for him in other ways. My son's mother and I still made the major parenting decisions. For Hunter and me, those were very happy months. We had alternate weeks to devote exclusively to each other, and we had supportive groups of friends, both straight and gay. We had been living together for six months when it became evident that, profes-sionally, there was little future for either of us in the city where we lived. Furthermore, we wanted to live in an urban environ-ment more receptive to our lifestyle. I was offered an excellent job opportunity in Washington D.C. We decided that I should accept the job and that we would both move there. In consid-ering the move, the question of how to maintain a shared role in parenting weighed heavily on my mind. I knew there was little chance of my former wife moving to Washington. The only solution that she and I could agree on was for my son to fly to Washington every other weekend and spend most vaca-tions there as well.

This arrangement left him feeling abandoned and left me wanting to cram two weeks of parenting and love into alternate weekends. The move was disruptive for everyone. Hunter seemed unable to replace the supportive group of friends we left behind. We had more time together than ever before, but there seemed to be little focus to our relationship. At the beginning of the next school year, my former wife and my son moved to Washington, and we resumed alternate weeks of parenting. Several months later, Hunter and I separated. My son expressed no feelings over this change. In fact, he delighted in being able to have my full attention! During the summers, my son spends much of his time with his grandparents. It wasn't until then that I felt comfortable dating other men. After the separation I worried about what signs of affection for another man would do to my relationship with my son. I was also afraid that my fitness as a parent might be brought into question by my former wife if there were signs of a new relationship.

During that summer I met Nick, my present partner. Our relationship had a chance to grow for several months prior to my son's return. We have been in a committed relationship now for a year and a half, although we have not lived together. On alternate weeks, the three of us are together several evenings, with Nick staying over those nights. I find myself trying to reinforce the bond of friendship and love between us so that when he understands my sexual orientation, he will be able to draw on the strength of our relationship to weather what I anticipate may well be a difficult time. My greatest fear is that he will reject me and choose to live apart from me. This is the one fear that I think is unique to being a single gay father. I look forward to the day when this fear is history!

The first interview with Michael was conducted in 1980, when his son was seven years old—a time in his life when Michael worried if their relationship would endure his son's knowledge that his father is gay. We thought it would be interesting to contact Michael in January of 1990 and ask him to give us an update ten years later. His son was seventeen years old. The result of that interview is presented in Box 7–1.

Michael, whom we followed for ten years, is a good example of the kinds of research needed from gay fathers on a larger scale. There are virtually no longitudinal studies on gay fathers. What we know about these men, in fact, is very limited, and is drawn almost entirely from self-reports from the fathers them-

Box 7–1
A TEN-YEAR FOLLOW-UP OF THE CASE OF MICHAEL

Over ten years after writing the previous paragraphs, it seems that my life has now been through a complete cycle. Nick and I continued in our relationship for another year. With my attention constantly divided between Nick and my son, there seemed to be no balance possible in my life. As time went by, Nick and I grew further apart and the relationship quietly ended.

In a matter of months, I met Martin, who was eleven years my senior. Martin's twenty-year marriage was just ending. The fact that we both had children (Martin's were in college) gave us much in common. We quickly set up housekeeping and established the routine of a middle-aged married couple. With the apparent permanency of our relationship, my son became very jealous of Martin. He began to spend most of his time at his mother's house. I felt rejected and a great sense of loss. Through this experience, I began to admit the imbalance in my life and, as a result, entered therapy.

Among the issues to be dealt with was my progressive alcoholism. As I began to look at issues, my relationship with my son began to improve. With tremendous effort on Martin's part, he and my son formed their own relationship largely centered on their mutual love of football. They would spend long boisterous hours in front of the television rooting for their favorite teams.

At the end of our third year together, I stopped drinking. Our fourth year I spent struggling with what seemed to be a forest of issues in my life. With the help of therapy and Alcoholics Anonymous, I maintained my sobriety. The common denominator in my life seemed to be my need to please and take care of everyone but myself. I had very little self-esteem. The progress I made seemed to create distance between Martin and me. Much of what we had shared was based on our mutual negative life view. For me this had to change. Martin's unwillingness to make changes for himself resulted in my walking out of the relationship.

At about the same time, my son became the victim of physical abuse on the part of his stepfather. Because of this, he has chosen to live with me for the foreseeable future. We are both in therapy together and separately. We are trying to develop a healthy, honest relationship in which we are not codependent. My son is accepting of my being gay. I am open with him about my lifestyle and introduce him to the men I date. Some of his peers and their parents have been less accepting, so we are now more careful about sharing information.

For me to be the person (and the parent) I want to be, I must love, respect, and take care of myself. When this is happening, there is balance in my life. My son senses this, I know. As he matures, I see him as a more accepting and tolerant person than I am. He strongly senses the injustice surrounding gay-related issues such as AIDS, as well as racial issues.

I look forward to the time when there is a significant man in my life again. However, for the next several years, I want to live separately from any lover I may have. I need to give this space to myself. Because of the healing in my own life, the fear of rejection by my son (and other significant people) is much less. I know that if rejection were to come, I would survive because I'm now learning to live with and love myself.

---

selves. Large groups of gay fathers followed over a period of years in which they are given self-report inventories, interviews, observed with their children and other family members, and even given standardized personality tests, would provide us a stronger, more scientific knowledge base about this special population of men. This more scientific approach would enable the development of more efficient legal, social, and helping policies. In this chapter we will examine the state of the research in this area and how it can be refined.

Empirical Neglect

As with any new area of study, gay fatherhood has received little empirical attention, presumably because gay fathers are a difficult population to reach (Robinson & Barret, 1986). Another reason, however, is the traditional overall neglect of the role of fathers in the family and parenting literature. Margaret Mead's famous comment that "fathers are a biological necessity but a social accident" accurately reflects the limited role expected of men in families. This pervasive view resulted in the role of the father as unimportant in his offspring's development. Although it is believed that up to 25 percent of self-identified gay men father children (Harry, 1983; Miller, 1979b), the topic of gay fathers is perhaps the least discussed and researched area in the fatherhood spectrum. The apparent incompatibility of being both gay and a father has led to large-scale neglect by social scientists.

The fact that gay fatherhood is a sensitive area has further limited potential research activity. The social stigma surrounding the topic has resulted in sparse government-funded research and in many researchers avoiding this area for fear they will be labeled gay and their careers sabotaged. At some institutions across the country, the topic of homosexuality is not considered a bona fide area of research for tenure and promotion. In addition to the homophobic conditions, there are other practical considerations that have limited research activity in this area. The target group is difficult to reach, and obtaining representative samples is costly and time-consuming. Because of the inaccessibility of the target group, much of the gay father research takes the form of personal impressions or suffers from problems in sampling and research design. Thus the generalizations drawn must remain tentative and exploratory in nature.

State of the Research on Gay Fathers

In the late 1970s, the two important research areas of homosexuality and fatherhood merged from separate topics into one. The earliest accounts of homosexual fathers ranged from personal impressions (Clark, 1979; Mager, 1975; Voeller & Walters, 1978) to a handful of empirical investigations (Miller, 1978, 1979a, 1979b). Research on lesbian mothers also emerged at this time (e.g., Goodman, 1973; Green, 1978; Hoeffer, 1981; Kirkpatrick, Smith & Roy, 1981). Our survey of popular and professional periodicals unearthed a total of forty-two articles pertaining to gay fathers. The majority of these articles were either commentaries (n = 17, 41 percent) or popular press (n = 8, 19 percent)—such as *Life Magazine, Cosmopolitan,* or *Psychology Today.* Only sixteen articles (39 percent) can be classified as empirical research of gay fathers (see Table 7–1). This figure is de-

Table 7-1
Demographic and Methodological Characteristics of Gay Father Research

Study	Sample Size	Sample Source	Age	Method	Locale	Design
			Descriptive Noncomparative Studies			
Bozett (1980, 1981a, 1981b)	18	support group	R = 28–51	interviews	West	convenience
Dunne (1987)	7	support group	M = 43	clinical observation	Northeast	convenience
Miller (1978, 1979a, 1979b)	40	snowball	R = 24–64	interviews	cross-national U.S. & Canada	convenience
Skeen & Robinson (1984)	30	support group	M = 41.4	questionnaires	national	convenience
Turner, Scadden, & Harris (1989)	10	support group	Mdn = 39	questionnaires	West	convenience
Wyers (1987)	32	advertising	M = 40.1	interviews	Northwest	convenience

Studies Comparing Gay Fathers and Heterosexual Parents

Bigner & Jacobsen (1989a, 1989b)	33	support group	M = 40	questionnaires	West	convenience
Harris & Turner (1986)	10	advertising & support group	Mdn = 39	questionnaires	West	convenience
Scallen (1982)	30	support group	Ukn	questionnaires	West	convenience
Robinson & Skeen (1982) and Skeen & Robinson (1985)	30	support group	41.4	questionnaires	national	convenience

Note: M = mean, Mdn = Median, R = Range, Ukn = unknown

ceptively inflated in regard to the actual number of studies that have been conducted, however. In many publications, researchers utilized the same sample in a series of different studies (i.e., Bozett, Miller, and Skeen & Robinson). Although this practice is not uncommon, upon closer scrutiny, it becomes clear that only eight distinct samples of gay fathers have been gathered: (1) Bigner & Jacobsen (1989a, 1989b); (2) Bozett (1980, 1981a, 1981b); (3) Dunne (1987); (4) Miller (1978, 1979a, 1979b); (5) Robinson & Skeen, 1982 and Skeen & Robinson 1984, 1985; (6) Scallen, 1982; (7) Harris & Turner, (1986) and Turner, Scadden, & Harris 1989; and (8) Wyers (1987). All these data bases contain small sample sizes. The largest is Miller's (1978, 1979a, 1979b) sample of forty gay men from large metropolitan cities in the United States and Canada.

As Table 7–1 indicates, sample sizes of this and other studies are too small and unrepresentative to place a great deal of confidence in the findings. The men studied tend to be in their forties, white, and middle class, and nonrandomized designs are routinely employed. Most of the studies were concentrated in one large city in the Western United States, each with its own distinct regional characteristics. Western U.S. cities such as San Francisco, Seattle, and Denver are overrepresented in this body of literature and contain higher gay populations where research subjects are more accessible. These urban areas are also known for their more liberal attitudes and lifestyles that are not typical of many other areas in the country. Exceptions are Miller's cross-national data and Skeen and Robinson's data from five different regions of the United States. Still, these sample sizes are low and randomization was not achieved.

Rigorous methodology is also lacking in the studies. Results (in 63 percent of the data-based studies) tend to be reported as descriptive data, and control groups are frequently missing (this occurred in ten of the studies). Where comparison groups are employed, only four published reports compare gay fathers with heterosexual parents, while two studies compare gay fathers with gay men who are not fathers. All of the samples were drawn from support groups and advertising that immediately contaminates the objectivity of the data. Gay support groups already clustered together for a common purpose are likely to be different from fathers who do not belong to groups or to gay fathers in the group who did not return their questionnaires. Openly gay parents in the research have established a publicly gay identification, whereas gay parents who maintain privacy are difficult to identify and have a whole set of different problems from openly gay parents.

Seven out of the eight gay father studies employ self-report data, either through mailed questionnaires or face-to-face interviews. This means that practically everything we know about gay fathers is what these men have told us. The entire body of findings rests on the self-reports of men who volunteer to come forth. This is perhaps the most serious problem of all, since what respondents feel or believe does not necessarily match their actual behaviors. Moreover, respondents may be highly motivated to participate in order to present themselves in a more favorable light to counter discrimination and victimization. Harris and Turner (1986), for example, noted that in their study, "The gay parents may have been particularly biased toward emphasizing the positive aspects of their relationships with their children, feeling that the results might have implications for custody decisions in the future" (p. 111). This tendency to unwittingly slant responses to produce favorable outcomes is a limitation of not only gay father research but of any research in which convenience samples (straight or gay) are employed.

Increased homophobia, legal discrimination, and violence against gay men as a blacklash from the AIDS epidemic will no doubt have the effect of driving many potential research subjects back into the closet, thereby setting back scientific investigation in this area. Until such time that our society is more conducive to better-quality research, we must continue to rely on those few pioneer reports discussed herein that are available to us.

The implications of this analysis are clear. The profile we use to understand and describe gay fathers is far from conclusive. Clearly, the literature has improved, after 1982, in the utilization of comparison groups and a more diverse, nationwide sampling. Still, until researchers can obtain larger, more representative samples that employ more sophisticated research designs, caution must be exercised in making sweeping generalizations about gay fathers and their families. Meanwhile, it is possible to make only limited speculations from some indirect sources and from a handful of direct sources that pave the way for future inquiry.

State of the Research on Children of Gay Fathers

Only two studies, not included in Table 7–1, address children of gay fathers (Green, 1978; Weeks, Derdeyn, & Langman, 1975). In both studies researchers gave psychological tests to children. The findings from this testing have been used to support the notion that a parent's homosexuality has little bearing on the child's sexual orientation. Our interviews with children also support this finding. Still, the problem is that the observations of Weeks and his colleagues are based on clinical assessments of only two children. The Green study observed children of lesbian mothers and children of parents who experienced sex-change surgery. None of the parents in that sample were classified as gay fathers. Findings from these two sources and other studies of lesbian mothers (e.g., Goodman, 1973, Hoeffer, 1981; Kirkpatrick, Smith & Roy, 1981) are frequently generalized to include the gay father's children, despite the fact that important differences exist between transsexuals and gay men as well as between gay men and lesbians.

We know, from existing findings, for example, that lesbian mothers have significantly lower incomes than gay fathers, have more multiple marriages, are less likely to live with a lover, are more likely to tell their children themselves of their homosexuality, and are more likely to have trouble reconciling their gay and parenting roles (Turner, Scadden & Harris, 1989). These basic differences could account for different developmental outcomes among the offspring of gay men. The limited information about the offspring of gay fathers comes from interviews with adolescent and adult children (Miller, 1979a). Those results were based on subjective self-reports of the respondents and contained no objective assessments. Thus, there are essentially no data on the direct observation of young children of gay fathers.

Suggestions for Future Research

The sampling and methodological flaws previously discussed have been largely overlooked due to a need for creating a data base. However, sampling and methodological specificity will become increasingly important as more researchers begin to address this field of study. A number of actions can be taken that will improve the quality of research on gay fathers and ultimately our understanding of them.

ADDITIONAL RESEARCH

An increase is needed in the sheer quantity of studies on gay fatherhood that include the gay father family as a system of inquiry. Direct sources of research assessment should be used, with gay fathers never used as voices for their children or spouses. Nothing is known about the maternal or paternal grandparents' thoughts and feelings about having grandchildren reared by a gay son or son-in-law. A beginning is needed in this area.

STRONGER METHODOLOGICAL APPROACHES

Researchers in the area of gay fathers need to strengthen their methodological approaches. As long as research studies on gay fathers are riddled with procedural problems, potential positive statements will be weakened. Lack of rigorous research only provides ammunition for critics to continue to refute current findings, wield homophobic attitudes, and victimize the target population. To develop more sophisticated research inquiries that will lend credence to gay fatherhood as a legitimate area of study and a viable parenting style, we recommend the following steps:

- Crosschecks should be provided in future questionnaire studies to monitor social-desirability responses.
- Reliance on unrepresentative sampling of gay fathers in one exclusive urban area will no longer suffice. Subjects should

be selected from diverse areas of the country and from more randomized populations.

- It is essential that future research employ a systems-oriented approach and assess perceptions and behaviors of spouses, fathers, children, and grandparents. Gay fathers' perceptions need to be compared with those of their children, spouses, and grandparents. Maintaining an ecological focus is crucial as gay fathers are observed interacting in their natural environments. Researchers need multivariate designs that will provide data on the interaction of significant variables that impact on gay fathers and their families.

- Multimethod approaches to data collection in which observational and clinical techniques are used in conjunction with the traditional self-report and interview techniques will yield more sophisticated data, undergird the research with strong systematic nonself-report information, and lead to a better understanding of gay fathers. This approach will also enable study of actual behaviors rather than reliance on perceptions.

- Larger samples and more rigorous research designs in gay father research are necessary with gay nonfathers and heterosexual fathers used as control groups.

Relevant Comparison Groups

Rather than investigating samples of gay fathers for descriptive and noncomparative purposes, designs should contain relevant comparison groups to advance what we already know in this area. For example, more information is needed on possible social and psychological differences between gay fathers and their nonfather contemporaries and between gay fathers and heterosexual fathers.

Research questions might include the following: Are there differences between gay fathers who never marry and those who do? Are there differences between the men who are intensely involved in the fathering experience and those who remain aloof? How do gay fathers interact with their children compared with heterosexual fathers? What are the differences between children reared in one gay father family configuration (as discussed in Chapter 2) as compared with another, and what conditions can be attributed to those differences? Is one family configuration more advantageous for the child's development than another? What factors differentially influence the parenting practices of men in these comparison groups? What is the social and psychological aftermath experienced by gay fathers who, after fathering children, are denied contact with mother and baby? What are the different concerns faced by a twenty-seven-year-old gay father with preschool children and a fifty-year-old gay father whose children are out of the nest?

The body of research that exists on divorce and stepparenting for heterosexual families is still in its infancy, and little is known about these family types. Research on the added dimension of gay father stepfamilies and the other family configurations is nonexistent. The research paradigms used in divorce, single-parent, and stepfamily research could be replicated with gay fatherhood as an independent variable.

LONGITUDINAL STUDIES

Long-term studies are needed to follow gay fathers over time to assess attitudinal and behavioral differences in fathering and family life. Future longitudinal investigations should also address the kinds of long-term adjustments and adaptions that are made or need to be made by gay fathers. The transition to fatherhood as well as effects on children can be monitored at different age levels. Those subjects who are first-time fathers in young adulthood and lose contact with mother and baby can be studied as older men to measure potential psychological aftereffects.

DEVELOPMENTAL OUTCOMES OF CHILDREN

There is virtually no information on the developmental outcomes of young children living in gay father households. The body of research on the gay father's children is woefully incomplete and for the most part relies heavily on data from lesbian mothers and their children (e.g., Goodman, 1973; Hoeffer, 1981; Kirkpatrick, Smith & Roy, 1981) or from men who have had sex-change surgery (Green, 1978).

While we know that the sexuality of children of gay fathers is not persuaded and that these children are sexually abused no more than children from heterosexual homes, many unanswered questions remain. Long-term studies on the psychological and social impact of living with a gay father need to be conducted in relation to the child's self-concept and social relationships with peers. We need to know the pros and cons children experience when they are reared between two worlds—one gay and one straight. This information cannot be objectively judged by interview and questionnaire approaches used in the past.

Children as Intermediaries

We need to know of the transgenerational family dynamics that occur in gay father families. What, for instance, is the nature of interaction between children of gay fathers with both sets of grandparents? Michael reported in his update that his son intervened on his behalf when the grandparents (Michael's parents) made critical remarks about Michael's homosexuality. Some of our other case interviews suggest that children become intermediaries between gay fathers and other hostile family members or between fathers and teachers and other adults in the community. But how common is this tendency? A more systematic approach to the intermediary roles children of gay fathers play would provide useful answers.

Tips for Practitioners

In choosing theoretical guidelines for the study of gay fathers, social workers, teachers, family counselors, and the clergy must continue to explore alternatives to Freudian theory, which emphasizes pathological behavior. Although a promising beginning has been made in this direction, a good deal still needs to be done. Clearly, antiquated Freudian themes continue to dominate the thinking of many practitioners. Simplistic Freudian explanations from the turn of the century will not work in our complex society of the 1990s.

Enlightened practitioners can disseminate nonprejudicial information to the general public by writing for the popular press or speaking in public forums. Contact with legislators at both local and national levels would also be a catalyst for attitude change.

Helping professionals can cooperate, within legal and ethical confidentiality constraints, with researchers of gay fatherhood. Funding agencies, social agencies, and researchers can combine their resources to improve the information base about gay fathers. Funding agencies can also be more sensitive to the many obstacles that researchers encounter in attempting to gather meaningful information. Health clinics, residential homes for children, hospitals, public schools, day care centers, and other human services agencies that have gay parents as clients can cooperate with research efforts. Social agencies can also be more cooperative with researchers. It is important for agencies to protect their clients from exploitation. Well developed research activities conducted by ethical professionals, however, can help erase common myths, homophobic attitudes, and ultimately improve the nature and quality of medical, legal, custodial, and other human services rendered to gay fathers.

References

Bigner, J. & Jacobsen, R. B. (1989a). Parenting behaviors of homosexual and heterosexual fathers. *Journal of Homosexuality, 18,* 173–186.

Bigner, J. & Jacobsen, R. B. (1989b). The value of children for gay versus homosexual fathers. *Journal of Homosexuality, 18,* 163–172.

Bozett, F. W. (1981a). Gay fathers: Evolution of the gay-father identity. *American Journal of Orthopsychiatry, 51,* 552–559.

Bozett, F. W. (1981b). Gay fathers: Identity conflict resolution through integrative sanctioning. *Alternate Lifestyles, 4,* 90–107.

Bozett, F. W. (1980). Gay fathers: How and why they disclose their homosexuality to their children. *Family Relations, 29,* 173–179.

Clark, D. (1979). Being a father. In B. Berzon & R. Leighton (eds.), *Positively gay.* Millbrae, CA: Celestial Arts.

Dunne, E. J. (1987). Helping gay fathers come out to their children. *Journal of Homosexuality, 14*, 213–222.

Goodman, B. (1973). The lesbian mother. *American Journal of Orthopsychiatry, 43*, 283–284.

Green, R. (1978). Sexual identity of 37 children raised by homosexual or transsexual parents. *American Journal of Psychiatry, 135*, 692–697.

Harris, M. B. & Turner, P. H. (1986). Gay and lesbian parents. *Journal of Homosexuality, 12*, 101–113.

Harry, J. (1983). Gay male and lesbian relationships. In E. D. Macklin & R. H. Rubin (eds.), *Contemporary Families and Alternate Lifestyles: Handbook on Research and Theory.* Beverly Hills: Sage, 216–234.

Hoeffer, B. (1981). Children's acquisition of sex-role behavior in lesbian-mother families. *American Journal of Orthopsychiatry, 51*, 536–544.

Kirkpatrick, M., Smith, C. & Roy, R. (1981). Lesbian mothers and their children. *American Journal of Orthopsychiatry, 51*, 545–551.

Mager, D. (1975). Faggot fathers. In K. Jay & A. Young (eds.), *After You're Out.* New York: Quick Fox.

Miller, B. (1979a). Gay fathers and their children. *The Family Coordinator, 28*, 544–552.

Miller, B. (1979b). Unpromised paternity: The lifestyles of gay fathers. In M. Levine (ed.), *Gay Men.* New York: Harper & Row.

Miller, B. (1978). Adult sexual resocialization: Adjustments toward a stigmatized identity. *Alternate Lifestyles, 1*, 207–234.

Robinson, B. E. & Barret, R. L. (1986). *The Developing Father.* New York: Guilford.

Robinson, B. E. & Skeen, P. (1982). Sex-role orientation of gay fathers versus gay nonfathers. *Perceptual and Motor Skills, 55*, 1055–1059.

Scallen, R. (1982). An investigation of paternal attitudes and behavior in homosexual and heterosexual fathers. Doctoral dissertation. Los Angeles: California School of Professional Psychology. *Dissertation Abstracts International, 42*, 3809B.

Skeen, P. & Robinson, B. E. (1985). Gay fathers' and gay nonfathers' relationships with their parents. *Journal of Sex Research, 21*, 86–91.

Skeen, P. & Robinson, B. E. (1984). Family backgrounds of gay fathers: A descriptive study. *Psychological Reports, 54*, 999–1005.

Turner, P. H., Scadden, L. & Harris, M. B. (1990). Parenting in gay and lesbian families. *Parenting Studies*, in press.

Voeller, B. & Walters, J. (1978). Gay fathers. *The Family Coordinator, 27*, 149–157.

Weeks, R. B., Derdeyn, A. P., & Langman, M. (1975). Two cases of children of homosexuals. *Child Psychiatry and Human Development, 6*, 26–32.

Wyers, N. L. (1987). Lesbian and gay spouses and parents: Homosexuality in the family. *Social Work, 32*, 143–148.

Appendix:
Resources on Gay Fathers

THE CASE OF PHILLIP

I am fifty-two years old. I got married when I was twenty-nine, and I was married for eighteen years. I have one son who is twenty-one. I got married because I was in love and wanted very badly to have children. I married a very beautiful woman. We had five miscarriages before our son was born. I think sometimes you're blessed when you're gay and don't show outward signs of homosexuality. I don't, and so I wasn't labeled like a lot of gay men. But then you have to consider the era I grew up in and the coastal Southern city of 50,000 people where I was born. I didn't know another gay person, or even the term "gay." There were the usual derogatory terms like "homosexual" or "queer." And I didn't know anybody else who was gay. So I didn't know I was gay when I was young, but I knew I had feelings toward men, although I didn't act on them. Because of the few encounters of homosexuality in junior high school when everybody was involved in it, including the jocks, you figure that part of it is okay. It was part of the game. But I knew I had more than a casual interest in the game. I just stuffed those feelings. There were no models, I didn't know anything about it. I didn't know there were gay people who lived together all their lives. I didn't think about it any more than I had to, and I sublimated like crazy. Now that I look back, I realize that a lot of things I was involved in was stuffing feelings. I was in everything. I filled every moment of time with every type of extracurricular and social activity, got elected to everything, and chaired every committee. I still do it today because I enjoy it, but back then I kept so busy so that I wouldn't deal with that.

My marriage was to be forever, and of course it lasted for eighteen years, which was better than average. And to our friends, we had the perfect marriage. Within the marriage there was very little conflict. We had our problems, but they would never have shattered the marriage. I would go six months without having sex with another man or even thinking about it. But I would dream about it a lot, which should have told me something about what my unconscious was telling me. I would go through these disciplines. I was a Christian minister, and I felt that homosexuality was wrong. I thought the will could overcome anything, so I would try to will it out of my being. I was a minister of a 500 member congregation and went as far as one could go from the standpoint of being successful. I always had lucrative pastorates and got all kinds of good strokes. I was a big leader in our denomination—I even had buildings named after me. One thing I didn't do was condemn homosexuality in the pulpit, though. And lots of homosexual people came to me to confess. I always told them what I didn't believe myself. I would tell them, "God made you this way. You've just got to live with yourself and get help to be who you are."

I used people as sexual partners. This became something unbearable that I would do—a real cheap pick-up type of thing. Finally, in 1975, I met a person that I liked as a friend, not sexually, although it started as a sexual encounter. I liked the person tremendously. He was a professional man who had been married and divorced. I actually told him who I was and what I did for a living. Before that point I had never told anybody that I was involved with sexually who I was. I had these two distinct lives. I don't know why I didn't go crazy.

Getting to the point of being able to accept myself and my homosexuality was very slow and painful. I never want to go through it again. I had reached the pinnacle of my work at forty-eight years old and had a child ready to go to college in two years. The empty nest syndrome was coming up, with fifteen more years before retirement. All kinds of things started coming up. I had one brief encounter with somebody that I felt romantically inclined toward, but I cut that off immediately. I didn't want to have the problem exacerbated by having someone that I cared about. Along the way, the one friend to whom I revealed who I was helped me. Occasionally, I would have an opportunity to socially be with professional gay friends, some married and some not, where I felt comfortable and I was myself—my *true* self—when all those years, I hadn't been. That was really very hard to deal with. My wife began to realize something was wrong but didn't know what. We had everything in terms of lifestyle, always in front of the public. I was having a hard time being perceived as one person and actually being another. I would get all these honors. I got an honorary doctorate from Furman University primarily for religious purposes for having founded a hospice. I literally experienced almost a psychotic episode. When they put the hood around my neck after reading this glowing citation about Christian character and leadership skills, it was like somebody choked me. With the hood around my neck, I physically felt like I was being strangled. Another honorary service was coming up in another prestigious school, and I decided that I just couldn't sit on that platform and receive that award. All these things were acting independently of one another, yet it was coming toward a head-on confrontation. We ultimately confronted this, very painfully. We went for counseling. My wife was devastated by my revealing my homosexuality. Today we have absolutely no relationship. She sees homosexuality as a sin, and anyone who is involved in it has no good in them whatsoever. And I was really willing to be celibate. I could have been. I had gone until I was twenty-nine years old already. Four years of college, three years of graduate school, and a couple years of courtship, and I had never expressed this physically. But it became a test of wills. She began to say what I could and could not do, even to the ridiculousness of telling me I couldn't preach in a church where a staff member was gay. She made all sorts of unreasonable demands that I just could not handle, so I decided I would submit to intensive psychotherapy. I signed myself into a psychiatric hospital for fifty-two days. I told them as I was admitted that I didn't want to be "changed," but that I just wanted to process. During that process, I knew I would not be able to go back into any of my previous life. The facility was excellent. While in the hospital, I resigned from the pastorate. You would have thought that the pressure of all that would have driven me further into depression. Instead, I started getting better. Certain physical symptoms I had dealt with all my life went away. I always had a bad stomach, and I had diarrhea every day of my life. It all stopped in the hospital. It left in forty-eight hours after I openly said who I was and what I thought. I haven't had any physical problems since.

I had a very fine and kind Methodist minister come into my life. He called up and said this is who I am. He came to see me and talked about how he revealed his own sexuality, late in life, and about his own divorce and children. I began to read a lot of books, quit stuffing feelings, and looked at who I was. I realized that I could no more help my sexual orientation than I could the color of my eyes. And there was nothing in my background that you could tie Freud into. I had a great family relationship, a totally functional home, a father image that was strong and good, and a mother who didn't manipulate. I had a warm, loving father who would kiss me goodnight until I was grown and in graduate school and was as masculine as he could be. My mother let me go to California to work when I was in college. None of Freud fitted.

One of the things that I experienced was retrogression hypnotic therapy, which took me back to feelings and interests that I had when I was four and five years old. Our place at the beach in the summer came out, where I liked to see older cousins nude. I would think they were beautiful. I wouldn't touch or anything, but at five, I would leave the beach to go back to the house to watch my cousins shower. Don't tell me that was "learned." There was no sexual abuse or substance abuse in my life. I am convinced that homosexuality is biological, and that there are different degrees of homosexuality. The bell tolls on both sides. It is there, and everybody has some of both homosexuality and heterosexuality within them. We know that. And to deny it? Nothing other than self-preservation is stronger than our sexuality. If you stop to think about the fact that you take that and deny it. The psychiatrist said something very interesting and affirming. He said I had to have one of the strongest psyches in the world to have exceeded everybody's expectations, including my own, in my work to maintain a good marriage and carry this off and on at different times on the side, and not to have gone crazy.

After I resigned from the pastorate, I responded to anybody who wrote me a letter. I told them exactly what the situation was. That was part of my therapy. I hand wrote over 300 letters to my congregation. My wife, of course, talked a lot because she was angry and hurt. But I was not going to hide my sexuality from anybody. Anybody who came to see me at the hospital, I told the truth. I was not going to wait around for the rest of my life until I'm ready to die to come to terms with this. I had to process it now, strip it out, and walk around barefoot in it, and get it over with.

It was a terrible loss with my son. We are estranged today. I was as honest with him as I could be. I sat down with him and told him everything. He said he would always love me because I was his father. But when I was in the hospital, he distanced totally, which I can only attribute to one thing, that he was influenced by others. He's now twenty-one years old, and he's got to come to that conclusion. He's going to meet all kinds of people in the world. I happen to know that his best buddy is gay, but he doesn't know that. His best buddy has already said that he's going to tell him the year they graduate. He says he thinks my son is blind. My son was seventeen when I went through all this, and he was dealing with his own emerging sexuality. I don't think he is gay, but I'm sure he was threatened by this. The thing I've noticed is that the most masculine men, who were the most sure of themselves, were the most loving and accepting as I went through this.

Being a religious leader, I thought there would be total rejection. My family rejected me more than the community. My sister did. My mother was dying, so she knew nothing about it. My wife and son also rejected me. It hurts like hell, but I'm not going to let it kill me. I'm not going to let anything ever again—ever—push me to the place I was pushed four years ago. Nothing! Or anybody! I just will not. That was the thing I came out of the hospital with. I know who I am; I know the quality of person I am; I know the talents I have; I know the people I have constantly helped through a twenty-five-year professional career. I don't deserve that, and I'm not going to take it. But that had to come when I could accept myself, which was hard to do. There were no models. The only person at Wake Forest that I knew when I was in college was a gay guy who ended up jumping in Lake Cumo in Italy and drowning himself. And he was flamboyant and brilliant. But flamboyant to the point of being a caricature. And I thought, "God, I don't want to be like that. I have no desire to be like that."

I could have walked away out of my marriage years before all this happened. I had an excellent job opportunity that would have given me an executive salary. I could just have said, "I don't love you anymore," and I could have moved to a large city and done what I pleased and there would have been no hint of this. But I could not do that, just as I could not stop supporting my family. I send my family much, much more money than a judge would have ordered me to send to care for them. We divorced, and I told my wife what I would do. Nothing was mandated by the courts. I send them $750 plus half of my retirement benefits per month. I still send Christmas and birthday presents to my son. But I've never received any acknowledgments. I've had telephone contact with my wife, who has called and said there is something terrible missing, and why can't we get it back together. I've told her that I'm not going to go back into that and live a lie. I wish we could be friends. I wish that during family events when we needed to have both parents there that we could. At this point we can't because my wife won't allow it. I was not invited to my son's graduation. I would just like to have a relationship with my son because we did have a strong relationship. I took him to Europe with me twice and to ACC tournaments. We used to do lots of things together. It has been painful. Good Lord, it has been painful! And in the midst of all this, I resigned the pastorate, I came out to my family and friends, my wife and son rejected me, my mother died, I moved to another city, I made a job change, and I had a radical adjustment in financial lifestyle. It's a wonder I didn't go down the tubes. But I had a very strong Christian faith and some very good therapeutic help.

I no longer feel homosexuality is wrong. I can't change that any more than I can change the color of my eyes or if I'd been born left handed. I see what a lot of gay people do with it as wrong and that is promiscuity. A lot of it is socially induced because you cannot have normal friendships, particularly with people who have a dual nature. I've made peace with that. God made me, I love God, and God loves me. Where the wrong comes in is when we use people in sex. And I used people for a long time just for sexual gratification. I was so honest about everything else, that made it doubly hard. I met them in pick-up situations. A long look at a mall, cruise the park—all the cheap things. Of course, that was before AIDS was such a risk.

I would tell practitioners that if someone who is a gay father comes to them for help, they should affirm that man as a human being. Let them know they are all right, that they did not do this to themselves. "Are you going to beat yourself to death because you're not six feet tall, blue-eyed, blonde, and gorgeous with an I.Q. of 160?" We can't do anything about those things, just as we can't do anything about our sexuality. So the client needs to be affirmed. Some counselors can't do this because they can't handle it, and they screw some folks up badly by trying to twist them into something or mash them into a role that they cannot be mashed into. I've seen people become celibate, but I've never seen anybody change their sexuality. Maybe there's somebody floating out there who has, but I don't believe it. The other thing the practitioner can do is gently help them make their statements if they can. Help them assess their situations. For some men it would be better not to come out to their mates if it's going to cut them off from children. There's no real formula for every case. I would not have thought that my wife would have been so vicious, but she was. Life would have had a lot better quality for both of us had we had two parents bringing up our child rather than one. They made those choices, I didn't.

Today, at times I have nostalgia. I think, "Wouldn't it be nice to have this relationship with my son?" Then the reality that that's not possible sets in because I'm not going to be somebody that I'm not. The people that fell away, just fell away. Nobody did anything overtly. A few weeks ago, I went back to my pastorate and did a funeral. I was obviously nervous about doing it, but it was one of my dearest friends who wanted me to do it, and I was determined to do it. I didn't care what anybody thought. Everybody there knew—all 300 of them. It was one of the most affirming things that ever happened to me in my life. It took nearly an hour for me to shake hands with all the people who lined up to shake my hand after the funeral.

At fifty-two, things feel pretty good. If there had been someone waiting in the wings when I left my wife, I would have had a harder time adjusting to the aftermath. When I came out of the marriage, though, I was asexual for six months. I didn't think about sex. It just wasn't there. The last thing I thought of was that I would have somebody in my life as a partner. I didn't want that, I wasn't looking for that, and when it happened, it was like lightning struck. He is a divorced man with children, approaching middle age. Whether it lasts forever, I don't know. But it sure has been a good year. It's nice to have somebody who shares the same interests—a peculiar combination of the arts and sports, a combination of a person who's very brainy and very sexy.

Every man that thinks about doing what I did needs to assess whether he's willing to pay the price to get the goodies that "you are yourself." He'd better be willing to take lumps. "If you pick the roses, you're going to find the thorns." Today I feel like a totally different person. If someone told me four years ago that I would be as creative, productive, and happy as I am, I wouldn't have believed them. I look back on all those years, the majority of my life. Even though it was only four years ago, it seems like eons, almost like it happened to somebody else. I look at an old photograph of me with the governor of South Carolina and I think, "Who is that? What was that?" It's like an out-of-body experience. It's like floating up in the air, looking down, and watching this happen. If somebody waved a magic wand and I could step back to four years ago before the confrontations, I wouldn't do it. The loss of my child is very, very hard. It hurts terribly. And I'm sorry my wife and I can't be friends, but that's her choice, not mine. I want my child, but I wouldn't trade places. It is a rebirth to be able to be who you are!

Resources

This appendix contains books for adults and children, organizations, periodicals, audiovisuals, unpublished research reports, and a professional library for practitioners interested in research, counseling and social work, education, and the popular press—all pertaining to gay fathers.

A. Books for Adults

Many books have been written about and for gay fathers. Some books emphasize the gay parent, others focus on the offspring of gay and lesbian parents, while still others examine the parents of gay men and lesbian women. Readings in the following list have been organized by their emphasis on one of the following categories: general issues about homosexuality; gay and lesbian parents; married gay men; children of gay and lesbian parents; and parents of gay and lesbian children.

General Issues About Homosexuality

Bell, A. P. & Weinberg M. S. (1978). *Homosexualities: A Study of Diversity among Men and Women.* New York: Simon & Schuster.

Bell, A. P., Weinberg, M. S. & Hammersmith, S. K. (1981). *Sexual Preference: Its Development in Men and Women.* Bloomington, Indiana: Indiana University Press.

Brown, H. (1976). *Familiar Faces, Hidden Lives: The Story of Homosexual Men in America Today.* New York: Harcourt Brace Jovanovich.

Bullough, V. (1979). *Homosexuality: A History.* New York: New American Library.

Clark, D. (1977). *Loving Someone Gay.* Berkeley, CA: Celestial Arts.

Cory, D. W. (1951). *The Homosexual in America.* New York: Greenburg.

Curry, H. & Clifford, D. (1980). *A Legal Guide for Lesbian and Gay Couples.* Reading, MA: Addison-Wesley.

DeCecco, J. (1988). *Gay Relationships.* New York: Harrington Park Press.

Gonsiorek, J. C. (1982). *Homosexuality and Psychotherapy: A Practitioner's Handbook of Affirmative Models.* New York: Haworth Press. (This book includes therapeutic approaches, directions, and issues for working with gay men and lesbian women.)

Harry, J. (1983). Gay male and lesbian relationships. In E. D. Macklin & R. H. Rubin (eds.), *Contemporary Families and Alternate Lifestyles: Handbook on Research and Theory.* Beverly Hills: Sage, 216–234.

Hart, J. & Richardson, D. (1981). *The Theory and Practice of Homosexuality.* London: Routledge & Kegan Paul.

Hidalgo, H., Peterson, T. L. & Woodman, N. J. (1985). *Lesbian and Gay Issues: A Resource Manual for Social Workers.* Silver Spring, MD: National Association of Social Workers.

Humphreys, L. (1975). *Tearoom Trade: Impersonal Sex in Public Places.* Chicago: Aldine.

Isay, R. A. (1989). *Being Homosexual: Gay Men and Their Development.* New York: Farrar, Straus, Giroux.

Jay, K. & Young, A. (1980). *The Gay Report.* New York: Summit.

Kirk, K. & Madsen, H. (1989). *After the Ball: How America Will Conquer its Fear and Hatred of Gays in the 90s.* New York: Doubleday.

Malone, J. (1980). *Straight Women/Gay Men.* New York: The Dial Press.

Miller, B. (1982). Gay men's relationships with women. In D. David & R. Brannon (eds.), *The 49% Majority: The Male Gender Role.* Reading, MA: Addison-Wesley.

Moses, A. E. & Hawkins, R. O. (1982). *Counseling Lesbian Women and Gay Men: A Life-Issues Approach.* St. Louis: Mosby.

Rueda, E. T. (1982). *The Homosexual Network: Private Lives & Public Policy.* Old Greenwich, CT: The Devin Adair Company.

Weinberg, G. (1972). *Society and the Healthy Homosexual.* New York: Doubleday.

Woodman, N. & Lenna, H. (1980). *Counseling with Gay Men and Women: A Guide for Facilitating Positive Life Styles.* San Francisco: Jossey-Bass, 1980.

GAY AND LESBIAN PARENTS

Bozett, F. W. (1989). *Homosexuality and the Family.* New York: The Haworth Press.

Bozett, F. W. (1988). Gay fatherhood. In P. Bronstein & C. P. Cowan (eds.), *Fatherhood Today: Men's Changing Role in the Family.* New York: Wiley.

Bozett, F. W. (1988). Fathers who are gay. In R. Kus (ed.), *Helping Your Gay and Lesbian Client: A Psychosocial Approach from Gay and Lesbian Perspectives.* Boston: Alyson.

Bozett, F. W. (1987). *Gay and Lesbian Parents.* New York: Praeger.

Bozett, F. W. (1985). Gay men as fathers. In S. M. H. Hanson & F. W. Bozett (eds.), *Dimensions of Fatherhood.* Beverly Hills, CA: Sage.

Bozett, F. W. (1981). Fathers who are homosexual. In L. H. Gross (ed.), *The Parents' Guide to Teenagers.* New York: Macmillan.

Clark, D. (1979). Being a gay father. In B. Berzon & R. Leighton (eds.), *Positively Gay.* Millbrae, CA: Celestial Arts.

Gantz, J. (1981). *Gay Fathers: Some of Their Stories, Experiences, and Advice.* Toronto, Canada: Gay Fathers of Toronto.

Mager, D. (1975). Faggot fathers. In K. Jay & A. Young (eds.), *After You're Out.* New York: Quick Fox.

Marciano, T. D. (1985). Homosexual marriage and parenthood should not be allowed. In N. H. Feldman & M. Feldman (eds.), *Current Controversies in Marriage and Family.* Beverly Hills, CA: Sage, 293–302.

Miller, B. (1982). Resocialization in moral careers of gay husbands and fathers. In L. Richardson and V. Taylor (eds.), *Issues in Sex, Gender, and Society: A Feminist Perspective.* New York: D. C. Heath.

Miller, B. (1979b). Unpromised paternity: The lifestyles of gay fathers. In M. Levine (ed.), *Gay Men.* New York: Harper & Row.

Parrot, A. & Ellis, M. J. (1985). Homosexuals should be allowed to marry and adopt or rear children. In N. H. Feldman & M. Feldman (eds.), *Current Controversies in Marriage and Family.* Beverly Hills, CA: Sage, 303–311.

Paul, W., Weinrich, J. D., Gonsiorek, J. C. & Hotvedt, M. E. (eds.). (1973). *Homosexuality: Social, Psychological, and Biological Issues.* Beverly Hills, CA: Sage.

Robinson, B. E. & Barret, R. L. (1986). Gay fathers. In B. E. Robinson & R. L. Barret. *The Developing Father.* New York: The Guilford Press.

Scanzoni, L. D. & Scanzoni, J. (1981). Gay parenthood and marriage. In L. D. Scanzoni & J. Scanzoni. *Men, Women, and Change.* New York: McGraw-Hill, 235–261.

Schulenburg, J. A. (1985). *Gay Parenting: A Complete Guide for Gay Men and Lesbians with Children*. New York: Anchor Books.

MARRIED GAY MEN

Brown, H. (1976). Married homosexuals. In H. Brown (ed.), *Familiar Faces, Hidden Lives*. New York: Harcourt Brace Jovanovich.
Gochros, J. S. (1989). *When Husbands Come Out of the Closet*. New York: Harrington Park Press.
Maddox, B. (1982). *Married and Gay*. New York: Harcourt Brace Jovanovich.
Ross, M. W. (1983). *The Married Homosexual Man: A Psychological Study*. London: Routledge and Kegan Paul.

CHILDREN OF GAY AND LESBIAN PARENTS

Gantz, J. (1983). *Whose Child Cries: Children of Gay Parents Talk about Their Lives*. Rolling Hills Estate, CA: Jalmar Press.
San Francisco Bay Area National Lawyers' Guild. (1981). *A Gay Parent's Legal Guide to Child Custody*. San Francisco, CA.

PARENTS OF GAY AND LESBIAN CHILDREN

Bergstrom, S. & Cruz, L. (1983). *Counseling Lesbian and Gay Male Youth*. Washington D.C.: National Network of Runaway and Youth Services, Inc., 905 Sixth Street, S.W., Suite 612, Washington, D.C. 20024.
Borhek, M. V. (1983). *Coming Out to Parents: A Two-Way Survival Guide for Lesbians and Gay Men and Their Parents*. New York: The Pilgrim Press.
Fairchild, B. & Hayward, N. (1979). *Now That You Know: What Every Parent Should Know about Homosexuality*. New York: Harcourt Brace Jovanovich.
Federation of Parents & Friends of Lesbians and Gays. (1978). *About Our Children*. Los Angeles, CA: Federation of Parents & Friends of Lesbians and Gays. (A pamphlet written by and for parents who are struggling to understand and accept their gay and lesbian children.)
Griffin, C., Wirth, M. & Wirth, A. (1986). *Beyond Acceptance: Parents of Lesbians and Gays Talk about Their Experiences*. Englewood Cliffs, NJ: Prentice-Hall. (Based on the real-life experiences of other parents, this book lets parents know they are not alone in their pain and grief and helps them reconcile their child's sexuality and transform and deepen family relationships.)
Sauerman, T. H. (1984). *Coming Out to Your Parents*. Los Angeles, CA: Parents FLAG. (A pamphlet that presents questions gay and lesbian individuals should consider before coming out. The consequences of what to expect are also presented.)
Schaefer, C. E. (1984). *How to Talk to Children about Really Important Things*. New York: Harper & Row.

Silverstein, C. (1977). *A Family Matter: A Parents' Guide to Homosexuality.* New York: McGraw-Hill.

Switzer, D. K. & Switzer, S. (1980). *Parents of the Homosexual.* Philadelphia: Westminister Press.

B. Book for Children and Adolescents

Holbrook, S. (1987). *Fighting Back: The Struggle for Gay Rights.* New York: Lodestar Books and E. P. Dutton. (Written for children from ages twelve and up, this book focuses on the gay rights movement and how the gay community is dealing with discrimination, the AIDS crisis, and what the future holds; how gay individuals view themselves, what their parents and teachers think, and how attitudes toward homosexuality are changing are also discussed.)

C. Special Reports and Papers

This section includes special reports and papers that have been presented at professional meetings. These unpublished works have relevance for practitioners and researchers nationwide. Because they are unpublished, it was difficult to locate a comprehensive listing of research reports, but this list is a good sampling of what is available across the country.

SPECIAL REPORTS

Bigner, J. (1986). "Attitudes toward Parenting and the Value of Children: Straight Versus Gay Fathers." Unpublished paper submitted for publication. Ft. Collins, CO: Colorado State University.

Hoeffer, B. (1979). "Lesbian and Heterosexual Single Mothers' Influence on Their Children's Acquisition of Sex-Role Traits and Behavior." Unpublished doctoral dissertation. San Francisco: University of California.

Louis, A. J. (1986). "Homosexual Parents Families: Gay Parents, Partners, and Their Children." Unpublished doctoral dissertation. New York: Columbia University Teacher's College. *Dissertation Abstracts International, 46,* 9–A.

McCord, T. H. (1983). "Fathers, Sons, and Sexual Object Choice: A Multivariate Study." Unpublished doctoral dissertation. Fresno, CA: California School of Professional Psychology. *Dissertation Abstracts International, 43,* 3368–3369–B.

Riddle, D. (1977). *Gay Parents and Child Custody Issues*. (Report No. C6–012–219). Tucson, AZ: University of Arizona. ERIC Documents. Reproduction Service No. ED 147 746.

Scallen, R. (1982). "An Investigation of Paternal Attitudes and Behavior in Homosexual and Heterosexual Fathers." Unpublished doctoral dissertation, California School of Professional Psychology, Los Angeles. *Dissertation Abstracts International, 42,* 3809B.

Steckel, A. (1985). "Separation-Individuation in Children of Lesbian and Heterosexual Couples." Unpublished doctoral dissertation. Berkeley, CA: Wright Institute.

Wyers, N. L. (1986). *Lesbian and Gay Spouses and Parents: Homosexuality in the Family.* Portland, OR: Portland State University School of Social Work Special Report.

PAPERS PRESENTED AT PROFESSIONAL MEETINGS

Baptiste, D. (October, 1981). "Treating Gay Stepfamilies: A Challenge for Marriage and Family Therapists." Papers presented at the American Association for Marriage and Family Therapy. San Diego, CA.

Bozett, F. W. (1986). "Identity Management: Social Control of Identity by Children of Gay Fathers when They Know Their Father is Homosexual." Paper presented at the Seventh Biennial Eastern Nursing Research Conference. New Haven, CT.

Bozett, F. W. (October 16, 1984). The children of gay fathers: Strategies for coping with identity variance. Paper presented at the National Council on Family Relations. San Francisco, CA.

Bozett, F. W. (October, 1983). Gay father/child relationships. Paper presented at the National Council on Family Relations. St. Paul, MN.

Bozett, F. W. (October, 1982). Gay fathers: Social policy concerns. Paper presented at the annual meeting of the National Council on Family Relations. Washington, D.C.

Bozett, F. W. (October, 1980). Jealousy in gay father relationships. Paper presented at the National Council on Family Relations. Portland, OR.

Miller, B. (June, 1978). Stigma contamination: Attitudes and adjustments of women married to gay men. Paper presented at the Canadian Psychological Association. Ottawa, Canada.

Riddle, D. (August, 1979). Gay parents and child custody issues. Paper presented at the American Psychological Association, Montreal.

Robinson, B. E. & Skeen, P. (July 17, 1986). "Gay Fathers and Their Families: Victims in Homosexual and Heterosexual Worlds." Paper presented at Groves Conference on Marriage and the Family, London, England.

Skeen, P. & Robinson, B. E. (June 4, 1982). "Gay Fathers." Paper presented at Groves Conference on Marriage and the Family. Ocean City, MD.

Skeen, P., Robinson, B., Paguio, L. & Wallinga, C. (October 17, 1984). "What about Gay Fathers in a New Era?" Paper presented at the National Council on Family Relations. San Francisco, CA.

Wyers, N. L. (1984). "Lesbian and Gay Spouses and Parents: Homosexuality in the Family." Paper presented at the Annual Program Meeting of the Council in Social Work Education.

D. Organizations

This section details the major organizations concerned with gay parenting. The organizations have been divided into two types: resource organizations and professional organizations. Resource organizations provide such services as dissemination of information on homosexuality and gay parenting, methods of supporting homosexual children, legislative advocacy for gay and lesbian individuals, and other types of assistance for gay men and lesbian women. Professional organizations are national associations of professionals dedicated to the improvement of those who work in the area of homosexuality and parenting. These organizations generally charge membership dues, publish their own journals, and sponsor an annual conference where members gather for seminars, speeches, and workshops.

RESOURCE ORGANIZATIONS

Children of Gays
8306 Wilshire Blvd. No. 222
Beverly Hills, CA 90211
A national support group headquarters for children with gay or lesbian parents.

Children of Lesbians and Gays
P.O. Box 12501
Fort Wayne, IN 46863

Fathers Rights Association of New York State, Inc.
Empire State Plaza
P.O. Box 2202
Albany, NY 12220

Federation of Parents and Friends of Lesbian and Gays (P-FLAG)
P.O. Box 24565
Los Angeles, CA 90024
A support group for parents whose children are homosexual. The group has chapters in major cities in the United States where parents can work through their grief to acceptance.

Gay Activist Alliance
99 Wooster Street
New York, NY 10014

Gay Dads
P.O. Box 5323
Berkeley, CA 94705

Gay Fathers Inc.
334 West 87th Street, No. 8A
New York, NY 10024

Gay Fathers Unlimited
625 Post Street, Box 283
San Francisco, CA 94109

Gay and Lesbian Parents Coalition International, Inc.
P.O. Box 50360
Washington, D.C. 20004
Composed of gay and lesbian parent groups, this organization was formed to give support to homosexual men and women who are fathers and mothers or are contemplating parenthood and may be struggling alone. In addition, the coalition educates professionals and the general public to gay parents' special strengths and special concerns.

Kinsey Institute for Sex Research
416 Morrison Hall
Indiana University
Bloomington, IN 47405
Founded by Alfred Kinsey, the institute sponsors research and publishes findings in the area of sexual behavior. Much of its research has focused on homosexuality.

Lambda Legal Defense Fund
132 West 43rd Street
New York, NY 10036

Lesbian and Gay Parent Project
21 Bay Street
Cambridge, MA 02139

Mattachine Society of Washington
Box 1032
Washington, D.C. 20013

National Coalition of Gay Fathers
146 East 30th Street
New York, NY 10016

National Congress for Men
P.O. Box 2272
Southfield, MI 48037

National Federation of Parents and Friends of Gays (NF-PFOG)
8020 Eastern Avenue, N.W.
Washington, D.C. 20012

Sex Information and Education Council of the United States
1855 Broadway
New York, NY 10023
Disseminates information from the field of human sexuality.

Spouses of Gays
450 Sutter Street, No. 2100
San Francisco, CA 94109

PROFESSIONAL ORGANIZATIONS

Association of Gay Psychologists
210 Fifth Avenue
New York, NY 10010

National Association of Social Workers Task Force on Gay and Lesbian Issues
110 West State Street
Trenton, NJ 08608

National Caucus of Gay and Lesbian Counselors
Box 216
Jenkintown, PA 19046
A caucus of the American Association for Counseling and Development, this organization seeks to educate and sensitize the membership and leadership about lesbian and gay concerns.

National Council on Family Relations (NCFR)
1910 West County Road B, Suite 147
Saint Paul, MI 55113
NCFR is dedicated to furthering all aspects of family life, including homosexual families, in terms of program development, education, research, and counseling.

Pride Institute
14400 Martin Drive
Eden Prairie, MN 55344
The nation's first gay and lesbian affirmative center for alcoholism and chemical dependency treatment.

Society for the Psychological Study of Lesbian and Gay Issues
American Psychological Association
1200 Seventeenth Street, N.W.
Washington, D.C. 20036
A division of the American Psychological Association, the Society provides an official and permanent forum for the presentation of scientific data and the exchange of theoretical and clinical information on lesbian and gay issues.

E. Periodicals

This section highlights the major periodicals in the field that publish articles pertaining to homosexuality and gay parenting. The periodicals list is classified into three types: newsletters, professional journals, and popular press. Newsletters are published by resource and professional organizations to keep readers up to date. Professional journals are usually, but not always, sponsored by a professional organization and referred by experts in the field; their content tends to be academic and research-based in nature. Popular magazines are generally written for the layperson in a casual style and sometimes lack a sound scientific basis. Nevertheless, many of the magazines listed here publish articles by top experts in the field.

NEWSLETTERS

Division 44 Newsletter
SPSLGI, 3210 De Witt Drive
Los Angeles, CA 90068
Published by APA's Society for the Psychological Study of Lesbian and Gay Issues, this newsletter keeps readers informed of the latest social science research and legislation on gay parenting and gay and lesbian issues.

NCGLC Newsletter
Box 216
Jenkintown, PA 19046
Publishes accurate and comprehensive resources for counselors dealing with lesbian and gay lifestyles and encourages objective research into gay issues.

Our Voice
The Pride Institute
14400 Martin Drive
Eden Prairie, MN 55344
The newsletter about chemical dependency and treatment in the gay and lesbian community.

Partners
Box 9685
Seattle, WA 98109
A monthly newsletter to help gay and lesbian couples establish themselves within the community. It includes such topics as buying homes, raising children, and socializing.

SIECUS Newsletter
SIECUS
1855 Broadway
New York, NY 10023
This newsletter is published quarterly by the Sex Information and Education Council of the United States and serves as a forum on the latest research and news in the field of human sexuality.

PROFESSIONAL JOURNALS

American Journal of Family Therapy
Brunner/Mazel Inc.
19 Union Square West
New York, NY 10003
Publishes topics and issues for family therapists to help them improve family practice.

American Journal of Orthopsychiatry
Editorial Office
19 West 44th Street, Suite 1616
New York, NY 10036
Published quarterly by the American Orthopsychiatric Association, the journal is dedicated to informing public policy, professional practice, and knowledge production relating to mental health and human development, from a multidisciplinary and interprofessional perspective.

Archives of Sexual Behavior
Sage Publications
P.O. Box 5024
Beverly Hills, CA 90212
A quarterly journal devoted to exploring the changing patterns emerging—as alternatives to the traditional nuclear family—in marriage, family, and intimacy. Includes studies of homosexuality, singlehood, cohabitation, and communal living.

Family Relations
National Council on Family Relations
1910 West County Road B, Suite 147
St. Paul, MN 55113
Directed toward practitioners serving the family through education, counseling, and community services. It disseminates reports of experiences in these areas, provides leads for others to explore, evaluates work using innovative methods, and discusses the application of research and theory into practice.

Human Sexuality Update
The Haworth Press
149 Fifth Avenue
New York, NY 10010
This quarterly periodical provides current abstracts on human sexuality with reprint addresses, plus review articles and features on new products important for clinical practice, and extensive book reviews.

Journal of Gay & Lesbian Psychotherapy
The Haworth Press
12 West 32nd Street
New York, NY 10001
This quarterly journal is a practical, multidisciplinary professional forum for the exposition and discussion of issues relating to the use of psychotherapy with gay, lesbian, and bisexual clients. The goal of the journal is to help therapists work with gay and lesbian clients to help improve the quality of life and to foster effective, sensitive forms of psychotherapy for those gay and lesbian people who require emotional, psychological, or psychiatric support in managing their lives.

Journal of Homosexuality
The Haworth Press
12 West 32nd Street
New York, NY 10001
Devoted to empirical research on homosexual and social sex roles. This journal has become a primary source of information in the field.

Journal of Marital and Family Therapy
American Association for Marriage and Family Therapy
1717 K Street N.W., Suite 407
Washington, D.C. 20006
Published quarterly, this journal serves to advance the professional understanding of marital and family behavior and to improve the psychotherapeutic treatment of marital and family disharmony.

Journal of Sex Research
Society for the Scientific Study of Sex, Inc.
Box 208
Mt. Vernon, IA 52314
Published quarterly, this journal serves as a forum for the interdisciplinary exchange of knowledge among professionals concerned with the scientific study of sex.

Journal of Social Work & Human Sexuality
The Haworth Press
149 Fifth Avenue
New York, NY 10010
Devoted to social work roles in dealing with problems of human sexuality in social agencies, including problems of family planning, casework methods for concerns of sexual-related problems, and social issues.

Medical Aspects of Human Sexuality
Hospital Publications, Inc.
500 Plaza Drive
Secaucus, NJ 07094
Published monthly, this magazine presents controversial and timely topics that highlight the medical aspects of human sexuality.

Parenting Studies
Department of Child Development
Iowa State University
Ames, IA 50011
An international quarterly journal that publishes articles on issues of parenting including research on teenage parenting, case studies, reports on innovative programs, and models and commentaries on trends in parenting.

Social Work
Editorial Office, NASW
2 Park Avenue
New York, NY 10016
Publishes articles that have implications for social workers and other practitioners.

POPULAR PRESS

The Advocate
Box 74695
Los Angeles, CA 90004

In Unity
Metropolitan Community Church
Box 38098
Los Angeles, CA 90038

F. Audiovisuals

This section includes audiovisuals on homosexuality and gay parenting. These resources are organized by the type of audiovisual and includes 16-mm films, videotapes, audiocassettes, and filmstrips.

16-MM FILMS

Choosing Children. A film about lesbian women choosing to become mothers. Order From: Cambridge Films, P.O. Box 385, Cambridge, MA 02139.

David Roche Talks to You About Love. A blue ribbon winner at the American Film Festival, this film depicts one man's disappointments in love that transcend the gay community. Color, 22 minutes.

In the Best Interests of Children. A film about lesbian women who are also mothers and what that experience entails. Order From: Iris Films, Box 5353, Berkeley, CA 94705.

Michael, a Gay Son. Reveals the feelings and needs of a young man, his parents, and siblings when he tells his family that he is gay. This sympathetic portrayal will help professional and general audiences gain insight into the dilemmas facing gay men. Order From: Filmmakers Library, Inc., 124 East 40th St., Suite 901, New York, NY 10016. Color, 27 minutes.

Not All Parents Are Straight. This film profiles six families in which children are being raised by gay and lesbian parents. As many issues are raised, the film allows viewers to judge for themselves whether or not children are at a disadvantage. Order From: The Cinema Guild, 1697 Broadway, New York, NY 10019. Color, 58 minutes.

Sandy and Madeleine's Family. A story about a family where the mother is lesbian. Order From: Multi-media Resource Center, P.O. Box 439E, San Francisco, CA 94102.

Silent Pioneers. There are 3.5 million elderly homosexuals in America who have lived their lives as "silent pioneers," quietly paving the way for a younger, more vocal generation. This film introduces eight individuals who lived through an era when homosexuality was not tolerated and who battled constantly for self-esteem and survival in a "straight world." Especially important for counselors and other practitioners. Color, 42 minutes.

VIDEOTAPES

Parents Come Out. A video documentary that shows parents and their families struggling to understand, accept, and continue to love their gay and lesbian family members. The stages of acceptance are described and depicted in this videotape. Order From: P-FLAG, P.O. Box 640223, Department 44, San Francisco, CA 94164-0223.

We Are Family: Parenting and Foster Parenting in Gay Families. This video looks at what life is really like in homosexual families, with the focus on parenting and the well-being of the children. Two gay fathers tell of their efforts to create a secure environment for their sixteen-year-old foster son; two adolescent daughters tell of how they have accepted their father's homosexuality; and two lesbian mothers help their adopted eleven-year-old boy overcome emotional trauma of a disability and early neglect. Order From:

Filmmakers Library, 124 East 40th St., Suite 901, New York, NY 10016. Color, 57 minutes.

<h2 style="text-align:center">AUDIOCASSETTES</h2>

Counseling the Homosexual Person. Presents a broad background about homosexuality with specific counseling concern. Order From: NCR Cassettes, Box 281, Kansas City, MO 64141. Two audio cassettes, 2 hours.

G. Professional Library

This section provides an extensive bibliography of further readings for practitioners in the field who wish to pursue their study of homosexuality and gay parenting in more detail. The bibliography that follows is drawn from professional journals and is subdivided into several interest areas: research; law and custody; popular press; and counseling and social work.

<h2 style="text-align:center">RESEARCH</h2>

Allen, C. (1957). When homosexuals marry. *Sexology*, February, 416–420.

Beiber, I. (1969). The married male homosexual. *Medical Aspects of Human Sexuality, 76*, 81–82, 84.

Bigner, J. & Bozett, F. W. (1990). Parenting by gay fathers. *Marriage and Family Review*, in press.

Bigner, J. & Jacobsen, R. B. (1989a). Parenting behaviors of homosexual and heterosexual fathers. *Journal of Homosexuality, 18*, 173–186.

Bigner, J. & Jacobsen, A. A. (1989b). The value of children for gay versus heterosexual fathers. *Journal of Homosexuality, 18*, 163–172.

Bozett, F. W. (1990). Parenting by gay fathers: Problems and issues. *Parenting Studies*, in press.

Bozett, F. W. (1989). Gay fathers: A review of the literature. *Journal of Homosexuality, 18*, 137–162.

Bozett, F. W. (1988). Social control of identity by children of gay fathers. *Western Journal of Nursing Research, 10*, 550–565.

Bozett, F. W. (1984). Parenting concerns of gay fathers. *Topics in Clinical Nursing, 6*, 60–71.

Bozett, F. W. (1983). Gay fathers' disclosure of their homosexuality to their children. *Nurturing News, 5*, 6, 9. (Reprinted *Identity*, 1984, *4*, 5, 10).

Bozett, F. W. (1981a). Gay fathers: Evolution of the gay-father identity. *American Journal of Orthopsychiatry, 51,* 552–559.

Bozett, F. W. (1981b). Gay fathers: Identity conflict resolution through integrative sanctioning. *Alternative Lifestyles, 4,* 90–107.

Bozett, F. W. (1980). Gay fathers: How and why they disclose their homosexuality to their children. *Family Relations, 29,* 173–179.

Cleveland, P., Walters, L., Skeen, P. & Robinson, B. (1988). If your child had AIDS: Responses of parents with homosexual children. *Family Relations, 37,* 34–51.

Coleman, E. (1985). Integration of male bisexuality and marriage. *Journal of Homosexuality, 11,* 189–207.

Fishel, A. H. (1983). Gay parents. *Issues in Health Care for Women, 4,* 139–164.

Gochros, J. S. (1985). Wives' reactions to learning that their husbands are bisexual. *Journal of Homosexuality, 11,* 101–113.

Goodman, B. (1973). The lesbian mother. *American Journal of Orthopsychiatry, 43,* 283–284.

Green, R. (1978). Sexual identity of 37 children raised by homosexual or transsexual parents. *American Journal of Psychiatry, 135,* 692–697.

Harris, M. B. & Turner, P. H. (1986). Gay and lesbian parents. *Journal of Homosexuality, 12,* 101–113.

Harry, J. & Lovely, R. (1979). Gay marriages and communities of sexual orientation. *Alternate Lifestyles, 2,* 177–200.

Hays, D. & Samuels, A. (1989). Heterosexual women's perceptions of their marriages to bisexual or homosexual men. *Journal of Homosexuality, 18,* 81–100.

Hitchens, D. (1980). Social attitudes, legal standards, and personal trauma in child custody cases. *Journal of Homosexuality, 5,* 89–95.

Hoeffer, B. (1981). Children's acquisition of sex-role behavior in lesbian-mother families. *American Journal of Orthopsychiatry, 51,* 536–544.

Kirkpatrick, M., Smith, C. & Roy, R. (1981). Lesbian mothers and their children. *American Journal of Orthopsychiatry, 51,* 545–551.

Kurdek, L. A. & Schmitt, J. P. (1986). Early development of relationship quality in heterosexual married, heterosexual cohabiting, gay, and lesbian couples. *Developmental Psychology, 22,* 305–309.

Miller, B. (1979a). Gay fathers and their children. *The Family Coordinator, 28,* 544–552.

Miller, B. (1978). Adult sexual resocialization: Adjustments toward a stigmatized identity. *Alternate Lifestyles, 1,* 207–234.

Morin, S. F. & Schultz, S. J. (1978). The gay movement and the rights of children. *Journal of Social Issues, 34,* 137–147.

Riddle, D. (1978). Relating to children: Gays as role models. *Journal of Social Issues, 34,* 38–58.

Robinson, B. E., Skeen, P. & Flake-Hobson, C. (1982). Sex role endorsement among homosexual men across the life span. *Archives of Sexual Behavior, 11,* 355–359.

Robinson, B. E., Skeen, P., Flake-Hobson, C. & Herrman, P. (1982). Gay men's and women's perceptions of early family life and their relationships with parents. *Family Relations, 31,* 79–83.

Robinson, B. E., Walters, L. & Skeen, P. (1989). Response of parents to learning that their child is homosexual and concern over and AIDS: A national study. *Journal of Homosexuality, 18,* 59–81.

Robinson, B. E. & Skeen, P. (1982). Sex-role orientation of gay fathers versus gay nonfathers. *Perceptual and Motor Skills, 55,* 1055–1059.

Ross, M. W. (1979). Heterosexual marriage of homosexual males: Some associated factors. *Journal of Sex and Marital Therapy, 5,* 142–151.

Ross, H. L. (1972). Odd couples: Homosexuals in heterosexual marriages. *Sexual Behavior, 2,* 42–49.

Simari, C. G. & Baskin, D. (1982). Incestuous experiences within homosexual populations: A preliminary study. *Archives of Sexual Behavior, 11,* 329–344.

Skeen, P. & Robinson, B. E. (1985). Gay fathers' and gay nonfathers' relationships with their parents. *Journal of Sex Research, 21,* 86–91.

Skeen, P. & Robinson, B. E. (1984). Family backgrounds of gay fathers: A descriptive study. *Psychological Reports, 54,* 999–1005.

Skeen, P., Walters, L. & Robinson, B. E. (1988). How parents of gays react to their children's homosexuality and to the threat of AIDS. *Journal of Psychosocial Nursing, 26,* 7–10.

Skeen, P., Walters, L. & Robinson, B. (1989). How parents of gays react to their children's homosexuality and to the threat of AIDS. *Journal of Psychosocial Nursing, 26,* 225–230.

Strommen, E. F. (1989). "You're a what?": Family member reactions to the disclosure of homosexuality. *Journal of Homosexuality, 18,* 37–58.

Turner, P. H., Scadden, L. & Harris, M. B. (1990). Parenting in gay and lesbian families. *Parenting Studies,* in press.

LAW AND CUSTODY

Berry, D. W. (1983). Visitation—Avowed homosexual's visitation rights. *Journal of Family Law, 22,* 185–188.

Blodgett, N. (1984). Family feuds: Gays fight for custody. *American Bar Association Journal, 70,* 38.

Broomfield, A. M. (1984). Discrimination in custody within the family court. *Legal Service Bulletin, 9,* 127–130.

Clemens, M. A. (1984). In the "best interests of the child" and the lesbian mother: A proposal for legislative change in New York. *Albany Law Review, 48,* 1021–1044.

Doe vs. Doe. (March 31, 1987). Gay father wins visitation rights. *Chicago Daily Law Bulletin, 133,* 1.

Green, A. (1982). The best interests of the child with a lesbian mother. *Bulletin of the American Academy of Psychiatry and the Law, 10,* 7–15.

188

Gay Fathers

Haller, L. H. (1981). Before the judge: The child-custody evaluation. _Adolescent Psychiatry, 9,_ 142–164.

Harris, B. S. (1977). Lesbian mother child custody: Legal and psychiatric aspects. _Bulletin of American Academy of Psychiatry and Law, 5,_ 75–89.

Hitchens, D. (1980). Social attitudes, legal standards, and personal trauma in child custody cases. _Journal of Homosexuality, 5,_ 89–95.

Kleber, D. J., Howell, R. J. & Tibbets-Kleber, A. L. (1986). The impact of parental homosexuality in child custody cases: A review of the literature. _Bulletin of the American Academy of Psychiatry and the Law, 14,_ 81–87.

Landry, J. S. (1986). Homosexuality and the custodial parent in Virginia. _George Mason University Law Review, 8,_ 389–404.

Morin, S. F. & Schultz, S. J. (1978). The gay movement and the rights of children. _Journal of Social Issues, 34,_ 137–147.

Moss, D. C. (1988). Tougher time for gay's custody: AIDS further muddies already difficult waters. _American Bar Association Journal, 24,_ 74.

Reidinger, P. (1987). Child custody: Gay father prevails. _American Bar Association Journal, 75,_ 73.

Rivera, R. R. (1986). Queer law: Sexual orientation law in the mid-eighties; part II. _University of Dayton Law Review, 11,_ 275–398.

Shepard, A. C. (1984). A new right for lesbian "fathers"? Visit sought to lover's child. _National Law Journal, 7,_ 9.

Sherman, R. (November 30, 1987). Homosexuals struggle for parental rights; concern over AIDS often a factor. _National Law Journal, 10,_ 3.

Skoloff, G. N. (May 26, 1986). Today's "innovative" lifestyles become issues in custody cases. _National Law Journal, 8,_ 24.

Somerville, M. A. (1982). Birth technology, parenting and "deviance." _International Journal of Law and Psychiatry, 5,_ 123–153.

Susoeff, S. (1985). Assessing children's best interests when a parent is gay or lesbian: Toward a rational custody standard. _UCLA Law Review, 32,_ 852–903.

Uhl, B. A. (1986). A new issue in foster parenting—Gays. _Journal of Family Law, 25,_ 577–597.

Walter, D. (December 10, 1985). Supreme court: Historic test for Georgia sodomy law. _Advocate,_ 11.

Walters, L. H. & Elam, A. W. (1985). The father and the law. _American Behavioral Scientist, 29,_ 78–111.

West, J. G. (November 25, 1987). A question of custody: Batey case illustrates the problems in deciding who gets the kids. _Los Angeles Daily Journal, 100,_ 4.

Whittlin, W. A. (1983). Homosexuality and child custody: A psychiatric viewpoint. _Conciliation Courts Review, 21,_ 77–79.

Wilson, V. (1985). Homosexuality and child custody: A judicial paradox. _Thurgood Marshall Law Review, 10,_ 222–234.

Zuckerman, E. (1986). Second parent adoption for lesbian-parented families: Legal recognition of the other mother. _U.S. Davis Law Review, 19,_ 729–759.

POPULAR PRESS

Anonymous (1977). I married a homosexual (as told to Kitty Kelly). *Cosmopolitan, 183,* 190–197.

Epstein, R. (1979). Children of gays. *Christopher Street,* 43–50.

Fadiman, A. (1983). The double closet. *Life Magazine, 6,* 76–78; 80; 82–84; 86; 92–100.

Finn, J. (March 1984). Gay fathers: Caught between two worlds. *Single Parent Magazine,* 22–23.

Gengle, D. (1977). All in the gay family. *The Advocate, 224,* 33–36.

Green, R. (1978a). Children of homosexuals seem headed straight. *Psychology Today, 12,* 44–46.

Klaich, D. (July 1976). Parents who are gay. *The New York Times,* 34–42.

Maddox, B. (February 1982). Homosexual parents. *Psychology Today,* 62–69.

Montagu, A. (August 1978). A Kinsey report on homosexualities. *Psychology Today,* 62–66, 91.

Oddone, M. (June 10, 1980). When a child is homosexual. *Woman's Day, 52,* 168–171.

Robinson, B. E., Skeen, P. & Walters, L. (1987). The AIDS epidemic hits home. *Psychology Today, 21,* 48–52.

Shilts, R. (1975). Gay people make babies too. *The Advocate, 175,* 25.

Walter, D. (December 10, 1985). Troubled time for Texas gays. *The Advocate,* 11.

COUNSELING AND SOCIAL WORK

Baptiste, D. A. (1987). Psychotherapy with gay/lesbian couples and their children in "stepfamilies": A challenge for marriage and family therapists. *Journal of Homosexuality, 14,* 223–238.

Beane, J. (1981). "I'd rather be dead than gay": Counseling gay men who are coming out. *Personnel and Guidance Journal, 60,* 222–226.

Bell, A. (1972). Comment on homosexuals in heterosexual marriages. *Sexual Behavior, 2,* 46.

Berger, R. M. (1977). An advocate model for intervention with homosexuals. *Social Work, 22,* 280–283.

Bozett, F. W. (1982). Heterogeneous couples in heterosexual marriages: Gay men and straight women. *Journal of Marital and Family Therapy, 8,* 81–89.

Cleveland, P. H., Walters, L. H., Skeen, P. & Robinson, B. E. (1988). If your child had AIDS . . . Responses of parents with homosexual children. *Family Relations, 37,* 150–153.

Cramer, D. (1986). Gay parents and their children: A review of research and practical implications. *Journal of Counseling and Development, 64,* 504–507.

Devlin, P. K. & Cowan, G. A. (1985). Homophobia, perceived fathering, and male intimate relationships. *Journal of Personality Assessment, 49,* 467–473.

Dank, B. M. (1972). Why homosexuals marry women. *Medical Aspects of Human Sexuality, 6,* 14–23.

Dank, B. M. (1971). Coming out in the gay world. *Psychiatry, 34,* 180–197.

Dulaney, D. D. & Kelly, J. (1982). Improving services to gay and lesbian clients. *Social Work, 27,* 178–183.

Dunne, E. J. (1987). Helping gay fathers come out to their children. *Journal of Homosexuality, 14,* 213–222.

Gochros, H. L. (1978). Counseling gay husbands. *Journal of Sex Education and Therapy, 4,* 6–10.

Golombok, S., Spencer, A. & Rutter, M. (1983). Children in lesbian and single-parent households: Psychosexual and psychiatric appraisal. *Journal of Child Psychology and Psychiatry and Allied Disciplines, 24,* 551–572.

Hall, M. (1978). Lesbian families: Cultural and clinical issues. *Social Work, 23,* 380–385.

Lewis, K. G. (1980). Children of lesbians: Their point of view. *Social Work, 25,* 200.

Neisen, J. H. (1987). Resources for families with a gay/lesbian member. *Journal of Homosexuality, 14,* 239.

Ross, H. L. (1971). Modes of adjustment of married homosexuals. *Social Problems, 18,* 385–393.

Rudolph, J. (1988). Counselor's attitudes toward homosexuality: A review of literature. *Journal of Counseling and Development, 67,* 165–168.

Shernoff, M. J. (1984). Family therapy for lesbian and gay clients. *Social Work, 29,* 393–396.

Thompson, G. J. & Fishburn, W. R. (1977). Attitudes towards homosexuality among graduate counseling students. *Counselor Education and Supervision, 17,* 121–130.

Voeller, B. & Walters, J. (1978). Gay fathers. *The Family Coordinator, 27,* 149–157.

Weeks, R. B., Derdeyn, A. P. & Langman, M. (1975). Two cases of children of homosexuals. *Child Psychiatry and Human Development, 6,* 26–32.

Weiss, H. W. (January 1984). On gay fathers. *SIECUS Report, 12,* 7.

Winkelpleck, J. M. & Westfeld, J. S. (1982). Counseling considerations with gay couples. *Personnel and Guidance Journal, 60,* 294–296.

Wyers, N. L. (1987). Lesbian and gay spouses and parents: Homosexuality in the family. *Social Work, 32,* 143–148.

Index

AIDS (Acquired Immune Deficiency Syndrome): 122, 133, 134, 141; and acceptance of homosexuals, 101, 113; adoption of children with, 110; and attitudes toward, 57, 101, 125, 127, 129, 132, 133, 134, 135, 138, 141; and case studies of, 123–126, 126–128, 128–129, 130–131, 131–133; and counseling of AIDS patients, 64, 136, 137, 138, 139–142; and fear of disclosure, 127–128, 129, 132, 133, 141; and fear of infection, 40, 125, 127, 135, 140; and gay attitudes toward issue, 57, 128, 129, 135, 138; and impact on gay culture, 5, 133, 135, 138, 140; and medical care, 125, 134, 141; and parental response to, 107–108, 134–135; and sufferers of, 121, 122–123, 127–128, 129, 132, 133–134, 137, 138, 140, 141, 142; and treatment of, 122, 123, 134, 140, 141. *See also* AIDS and Gay fathers
AIDS and gay fathers, 64, 101, 110, 121–142; case studies of, 112, 121, 122–133; and children, 121, 124–125, 128, 129, 130–131, 132, 133; and counseling, 121, 127–128, 133, 135–138, 139–142; and ethics, 138, 141; and fear of disclosure, 127–128, 129, 132, 133, 138; and gay couples, 123–126, 130–131; and parents, 134–135; research on, 121, 153; and wives, 64, 112, 113, 127, 138, 141

American Psychiatric Association, and definition of homosexuality, 16–17
American Psychological Association, resources on gay issues, 178
AZT (azidothymidine), 123

Bisexual fathers, case of: and AIDS, 126–128; and sexual relationships, 126–127

Children: resources for, on homosexuality, 172; and sexual abuse, 42, 43, 80; and sexuality of, 40–41, 72, 81, 93; and understanding of homosexuality, 63, 172, 173
Children of gay fathers, 10, 32, 41–42, 63, 82, 91–94, 129, 133, 154, 165; and AIDS, 121, 124, 125, 128, 129, 130, 131, 132, 133; and case studies of, 41–15, 69–73, 77–79, 124–125, 165–168; and coming out experience, 82–88, 93, 146, 147–148, 165–168; and conformity, 77–78, 98–99, 165–168; and counseling of, 69–71, 90, 91–94; and custody decisions, 6, 7–8, 62, 64–65, 80, 129, 171, 173, 187–188; and the gay community, 9, 12–13, 23, 42, 78–79, 148; and gay step-parents, 9, 12–13, 67, 68, 69, 145, 146, 147; research on, 154, 156–157, 158; and sexual abuse, 8, 33, 42, 80, 158; and sexual identity of, 6, 8, 32, 40, 41, 42, 65, 79, 80, 81, 93, 100, 154, 158, 165, 173; and

About the Authors

ROBERT L. BARRET, Ph.D., is professor of counselor education at the University of North Carolina at Charlotte and a psychologist in private practice. His interest in fathering can be seen in his relationships with his three daughters and two sons-in-law, as well as in his professional writing. A co-author with Bryan Robinson of *The Developing Father,* Dr. Barret is currently on leave in San Francisco participating in research on psychosocial responses to HIV disease.

BRYAN E. ROBINSON, Ph.D., is professor of child and family development at the University of North Carolina at Charlotte. He has been involved in research on the general topic of fathering for the past ten years. He is an internationally known lecturer, and author or co-author of thirteen books. His research on children and families in crisis has been published in more than one-hundred journals and such popular magazines as *Psychology Today.*